LIFE APPLICATION BIBLE COMMENTARY

Life

APPLICATION®
Bible Commentary

JAMES

Bruce B. Barton, D.Min.
David R. Veerman, M.Div.
Neil Wilson, M.R.E.

GENERAL EDITOR: Grant Osborne, Ph.D.
SERIES EDITOR: Philip W. Comfort, D.Litt. et Phil.

TYNDALE HOUSE
PUBLISHERS, INC.
CAROL STREAM,
ILLINOIS

Visit Tyndale's exciting Web site at www.tyndale.com

Life Application Bible Commentary: James

Copyright © 1992 by The Livingstone Corporation. All rights reserved.

Contributing Editors: James C. Galvin, Ed.D., and Ronald A. Beers

Cover photograph of bridge and path copyright © by Alyn Stafford / iStockphoto. All rights reserved.

Cover photographs of woman with a laptop and man holding a pen copyright © by Dan Wilton / iStockphoto. All rights reserved.

Cover photo of man reading copyright © by Ronnie Comeau / iStockphoto. All rights reserved.

Interior illustration of hands copyright © 2004 by Tracy Walker. All rights reserved.

Library of Congress Cataloging-in-Publication Data

Barton, Bruce B., date
    James / Bruce B. Barton, David R. Veerman, Neil Wilson.
        p.   cm. — (Life application Bible commentary)
    Includes bibliographical references and index.
    ISBN 978-0-8423-2891-3 (soft cover)
    1. Bible. N.T. James—Commentaries. I. Veerman, David. II. Wilson, Neil S.,
date. III. Title. IV. Series.
BS2785.3.B375 1992
227.9107—dc20
                                                                                    92-17490

Printed in the United States of America

14 13 12 11 10 09
20 19 18 17 16 15

CONTENTS

Gospels

MATTHE...
MARK: betwe...
LUK...

ACT...

Paul's Epistles

ROMANS: about...
1 CORINTHIANS: about 49
2 CORINTHIANS: about 56—...
GALATIANS: about 49

1 THESSALONIANS: about 51
2 THESSALONIANS: about 51—...

EPHESIAN...
PHILIPPIAN...
COLOSSIAN...

1 TIMOTH...
2 TIMOTH...
TITU...
PHILEMO...

General Epistles

JAMES: about 49

1 PETE...
2 PETE...

JUD...

NEW TESTAMEN...

AD 30 — 40 — 50 — 60

The church begins (Acts 1)

35 Paul's conversion (Acts 9)

46 Paul's first missionary journey (Acts 13)

Jerusalem Council and Paul's second journey (Acts 15)

54 Paul's third journey (Acts 18)

Nero becomes emperor

58 Paul arrested (Acts 21)

61–63 Paul's Roman imprison- ment (Acts 2...

64 Rome burn...

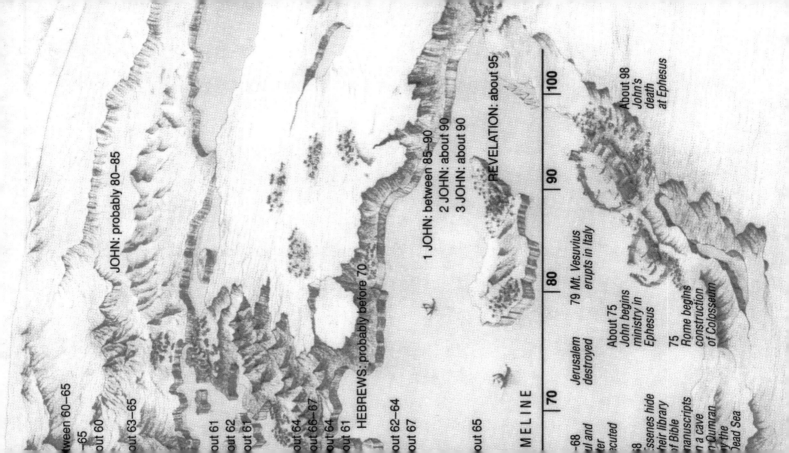

JOHN: probably 80–85

HEBREWS: probably before 70

1 JOHN: between 85—90

2 JOHN: about 90

3 JOHN: about 90

REVELATION: about 95

About 98 John's death at Ephesus

79 Mt. Vesuvius erupts in Italy

About 75 John begins ministry in Ephesus

75 Rome begins construction of Colosseum

Jerusalem destroyed

MELINE

| 70 | 80 | 90 | 100 |

ween 60–65
out 60
out 63–65
out 61
out 62
out 61
out 64
out 66–67
out 64
out 61

out 62–64
out 67

out 65

–68
ul and
ter
ecuted

8
ssenes hide
heir library
f Bible
manuscripts
n a cave
n Qumran
y the
ead Sea

FOREWORD

The Life Application Bible Commentary series provides verse-by-verse explanation, background, and application for every verse in the New Testament. In addition, it gives personal help, teaching notes, and sermon ideas that will address needs, answer questions, and provide insight for applying God's Word to life today. The content is highlighted so that particular verses and phrases are easy to find.

Each volume contains three sections: introduction, commentary, and reference. The introduction includes an overview of the book, the book's historical context, a time line, cultural background information, major themes, an overview map, and an explanation about the author and audience.

The commentary section includes running commentary on the Bible text with reference to several modern versions, especially the New International Version and the New Revised Standard Version, accompanied by life applications interspersed throughout. Additional elements include charts, diagrams, maps, and illustrations. There are also insightful quotes from church leaders and theologians such as John Calvin, Martin Luther, John Wesley, A. W. Tozer, and C. S. Lewis. These features are designed to help you quickly grasp the biblical information and be prepared to communicate it to others.

The reference section includes a bibliography of other resources, short articles on specific topics, and an index.

INTRODUCTION

In this epistle James addresses practical issues that are as current as this morning's newspaper, and yet his challenges are not dated. The timeless truth that James presents is that Christians must put their faith into action. The faith that Christians claim must be demonstrated in all the situations and circumstances of life—at work, at home, in the neighborhood, in church. Trials and hardships are not to be seen as hindrances to faith, but as opportunities to exercise healthy faith. Knowing God's Word is not enough. That knowledge must be applied to our everyday lives. Real faith is the application of God's truth to ourselves.

AUTHOR

James, son of Joseph and half brother of Jesus, also known as "James the Just."

What would it have been like to have Jesus in the family? Would Mary and Joseph wonder about their parental responsibilities? Would younger brothers and sisters be jealous, resentful, or awestruck? Would these children have seen anything special about their eldest sibling? Because there is so little information in Scripture about Jesus' early years, we can only speculate about what it would be like to have Jesus as a son or as an older brother. But such was the experience of James, the author of this book that bears his name.

We know very little about the relationship between James and Jesus. We do know, however, that the townsfolk who saw Jesus as a boy and young man rejected his adult claim to be the Messiah and were amazed at his wisdom and miraculous powers (Matthew 13:53-58). Evidently Jesus had kept a low profile in Nazareth. These skeptical neighbors included James in their description of Jesus' family: "Isn't this the carpenter's son? Isn't his mother's name Mary, and aren't his brothers James, Joseph, Simon and Judas? Aren't all his sisters with us? Where then did this man get all these things?" (Matthew 13:55-56 NIV; see also Mark 6:1-6).

At one point in Jesus' ministry, his "family" tried to stop him and "restrain him" (Mark 3:21 NRSV); presumably James was one of the family members who claimed that Jesus was "out of his mind."

Certainly Mary and Joseph knew who Jesus was. After all, they had heard the angels predict his miraculous conception (Matthew 1:18-25; Luke 1:38-56), and they had been present at his birth (Luke 2:1-7). In fact, "Mary treasured all these words and pondered them in her heart" (Luke 2:19 NRSV). They also had seen the boy Jesus grow and mature, with profound wisdom beyond his years (Luke 2:40, 49-52). Surely Mary and Joseph would have explained Jesus' true identity to the rest of the family. But James and the others (including Jude, the author of the book of Jude) remained unconvinced. John explains, "For even His brothers did not believe in Him" (John 7:5 NKJV).

Yet, just a few years after that incident, James became the leader of the church in Jerusalem (Acts 12:17). We don't know how James attained that important position (Clement of Alexandria wrote that he was chosen for the office by Peter and John), but clearly he was the leader. In fact, when controversy over Gentile believers threatened to divide the church, Barnabas and Paul met with the elders and apostles in Jerusalem and submitted to their authority with James as the moderator, spokesman, and announcer of the final decision (Acts 15:1-21).

Later, just before Paul's arrest, Paul brought money that he had collected for the church in Jerusalem on his third missionary journey to James and the rest of the elders and "reported in detail what God had done among the Gentiles through his ministry" (Acts 21:19 NIV).

That *this* James is the James mentioned earlier as Jesus' brother is confirmed by Paul in Galatians 1:18-19: "Then after three years, I went up to Jerusalem to get acquainted with Peter and stayed with him fifteen days. I saw none of the other apostles— only James, the Lord's brother" (NIV). Later Paul adds, "James, Peter and John, those reputed to be pillars, gave me and Barnabas the right hand of fellowship when they recognized the grace given to me" (Galatians 2:9 NIV). And he mentions that "certain people came from James" (Galatians 2:12 NRSV).

What changed James from a skeptical younger brother to a committed follower of Jesus and outspoken leader of the church? He saw his brother alive—he saw the risen Christ!

Writing to the Corinthians, Paul lists the eyewitnesses to the Resurrection: "For what I received I passed on to you as of first importance: that Christ died for our sins according to the Scriptures, that he was buried, that he was raised on the third day according to the Scriptures, and that he appeared to Peter, and then to the Twelve. After that, he appeared to more than five hundred of the brothers at the same time, most of whom are still living, though some have fallen asleep. Then he appeared to James, then to all the apostles, and last of all he appeared to me also, as to one abnormally born" (1 Corinthians 15:3-8 NIV). Jesus appeared personally to his brother James. Imagine that reunion!

Then, after the Ascension, we find James with the apostles, Mary, and others, praying continually (Acts 1:12-14) and waiting for the Holy Spirit as Jesus had told them to do (Acts 1:4-5).

This is James who describes himself as "a servant of God and of the Lord Jesus Christ" (1:1) and as a believer "in our glorious Lord Jesus Christ" (2:1). He is a man whose life was changed by Christ: a sibling turned servant; an antagonist turned apologist; a passive observer turned passionate follower.

What a wonderful opportunity we have, to read and study this book authored by God and written by one who had intimate contact with Jesus, who was an eyewitness to the ministry of Jesus and the beginnings of the church as recorded in the Gospels and in Acts.

It should be noted that other men named James are mentioned in the New Testament, and each one, at various times, has been proposed as a possible author of this book. These men include:

James, the son of Zebedee and brother of John (see Mark 1:19). This James belonged to the inner circle of disciples (with John and Peter). Certainly he would have had the prominence to be a biblical author. But he was executed by Herod in A.D. 44 (Acts 12:2), too early for the writing of this book.

James, the son of Alphaeus. This James was also one of the original twelve disciples. He is listed as an apostle (for example, Matthew 10:2-3) and quite possibly is "James the younger" (Mark 15:40).

James, the father of Judas, one of the twelve, not Judas Iscariot (Luke 6:16).

So little is known about these last two men (and any other unmentioned individuals named James) that they are not taken as serious candidates. The book begins with the straightforward statement, "James, a servant of God and of the Lord Jesus Christ" (1:1). The author assumes that his readers (called "the twelve tribes scattered among the nations") would know his identity. This James, the author, must have been someone well-known, with stature and authority in the early church. James, the brother of Jesus and the leader of the Jerusalem church, is the obvious choice. This is also the traditional view (since early in the third century) and the belief of most biblical scholars today.

According to Josephus, a first-century Jewish historian, James was condemned to death by the Jewish Sanhedrin in A.D. 62—just after the death of the Roman governor Festus (see Acts 24:27–26:32) and just before the arrival of his successor Albinus.

SETTING

Place. James probably wrote this letter from Jerusalem, where he lived. Jerusalem was the holy city of the Jews, the focus of the nation's political and religious life. In Jerusalem, Israel's greatest kings had reigned and prophets had ministered. And the temple was there. No matter how far they had been scattered, Jews all over the world looked to Jerusalem as their home and a symbol of God's presence among them. A reading of the last chapters of the Gospels and the first half of Acts provides an eyewitness view of the historical context of this book.

Religion. When Jesus walked the streets of this great city, he encountered Pharisees, priests, scribes, and other religious zealots committed to the purity of Judaism. Eventually these religious leaders plotted Jesus' death (see Luke 22:1–6), hoping to stop the spread of what they considered to be heresy. However, after the Resurrection and the coming of the Holy Spirit, the church was born—the disciples preached without fear, and thousands responded to the gospel message (see Acts 2:1–47; 6:7). The religious leaders reacted by working still harder to eliminate the church and obliterate any trace of Jesus' followers (see Acts 6:8–8:3; 9:1-2). Yet the Jerusalem church flourished through this persecution, with James as one of the leaders. Wonderfully, many Jewish religious leaders came to faith in Christ. The Jerusalem church included former priests and Pharisees.

In Jerusalem, the first great crisis of the church was successfully resolved through a church council (Acts 15); yet a few years later, in this same city, the apostle Paul was mobbed in the temple and arrested (Acts 21–22).

James wrote from a city in religious turmoil, with opposition from Sadducees, legalistic Pharisees, and a vengeful high priest. Christians were a persecuted minority.

Politics. During these times, Judea was under Roman domination. Herod the Great had been appointed king of the Jews by Augustus in 40 B.C., and he had chosen Jerusalem as his place of residence and reign. All the Roman governors ruled with power and intimidation, but they would often try to keep the peace by appeasing the religious leaders. Herod the Great had even constructed a magnificent temple. And Jesus was crucified when

Pilate bowed to public pressure (Matthew 27:15-26). But most Jews chafed under Roman rule and longed for the freedom and glory of the past. Uprisings and insurrections were common, and the land of Palestine continued to be an irritant to the Romans. Eventually Emperor Titus destroyed the city and the temple in A.D. 70.

James wrote from a city in political turmoil, in a land where the people lived under foreign rule, in occupied territory. Christians were powerless in the community. Often they had to accept their lot and live quiet testimonies within a hostile atmosphere.

Economics. In general, the Jews of Jerusalem were poor, although many of the landowners and religious leaders had wealth. In addition, tax collectors like Matthew (Matthew 9:9) and Zacchaeus (Luke 19:1-10) made financial gains by allying themselves with the Romans and exploiting their countrymen. Eventually, however, Jerusalem became desperately poor because of Roman greed and a terrible famine (Acts 11:28-30).

James wrote from a city with an unstable economy and from a people with very few material resources. The Christians in Jerusalem were poor.

Because of the conditions in Jerusalem, the Jewish believers were tempted to compromise their values and beliefs in order to escape persecution or to improve their economic situation. Certainly it would have been tempting to be secret believers, blending in with society and not causing problems. Or they might have been tempted to turn away from Christ altogether, giving in to the religious, political, and economic pressures.

Christians today face similar temptations. Although they may not be ruled by a foreign nation, believers are in a distinct minority in the world. Christ's teachings and commands continue to clash with society's values. And many Christians are persecuted socially, economically, and religiously because of their beliefs. Even in "Christian" countries, followers of Christ can feel alienated and ostracized. In an attempt to cope with the surrounding pressures, believers must resist the temptation to become secret Christians and silent witnesses.

Date of writing. James wrote this book about A.D. 47–49. There are several reasons for believing that the book of James was written early in the life of the church.

■ With James the brother of Christ as the author, the book would have had to be written before A.D. 62, the year of James's martyrdom according to Josephus.

■ The book does not mention the Jewish/Gentile controversy of the fifties and sixties. Remember, James was the moderator of the Council of Jerusalem, convened to consider this issue (Acts 15). This council is thought to have been held around A.D. 50. Paul spent much time discussing the problem of the Judaizers in his letters.

■ This letter has no mention of the apostle Paul or allusions to his writings. It is probable, therefore, that it was written before Paul's rise to great prominence in the church.

■ James does not discuss false teachings, another later issue in the church and a prominent theme in the writings of Paul, Peter, Jude, and John.

The book of James was written after the death of Stephen (A.D. 35), the persecution that caused many of the Jerusalem believers to flee for their lives, the conversion of Paul (A.D. 35), and the death of James the apostle (A.D. 44).

It was written before the Council of Jerusalem (A.D. 50), Paul's second and third missionary journeys (A.D. 50–52, 53–57), Paul's final imprisonment and martyrdom (c. A.D. 67), and the destruction of Jerusalem by Titus (A.D. 70).

Some have argued for a late date by another author because of the excellent Greek used in the book. James's natural language would have been Aramaic, and he probably would not have been fluent in good Hellenistic Greek. It is possible, however, that James, like Paul (see Colossians 4:18) used a "secretary" to translate his words into Greek, the language of world trade and the appropriate choice to reach those scattered among the nations.

James wrote to Jewish Christians in the first century. He also wrote to us, today, who are also "scattered among the nations." Although separated by nearly twenty centuries, the needs are much the same, and James's message still needs to be heard and applied.

AUDIENCE

"To the twelve tribes scattered among the nations" (1:1 NIV). Christianity is Jewish. That may seem like a contradiction, but it's true. Mary, the mother of our Lord, was Jewish, as was Joseph. So Jesus was reared in a Jewish home. And in his public ministry, Jesus came first to the Jews, God's chosen nation, calling them to repentance and faith. All of the original twelve disciples were Jews. Christianity began in the temple and synagogue, as seeking Jews found the Messiah.

Quite naturally, therefore, Jerusalem was the birthplace of the church. That's where Jesus was crucified and where he arose and later ascended. In Jerusalem the Holy Spirit filled the early band of believers. And that's where the apostles ministered. The Jerusalem church experienced explosive growth, with thousands responding to the gospel (Acts 2:41; 4:4; 5:14; 6:1, 7). Believers met in the temple courts and in homes (Acts 5:42), worshiping, eating, learning, and serving together.

Jesus had told his followers to spread the faith *beyond* Jerusalem to "Judea and Samaria, and to the ends of the earth" (Acts 1:8 NRSV). In the Olivet discourse Jesus predicted terrible persecution and the eventual destruction of Jerusalem (Luke 21:5-24)—Jesus knew that his followers would be scattered. The persecution began soon after Jesus' ascension. Whether or not these early Christians were ready, many of them were forced to spread throughout the Roman Empire (Acts 8:1). They traveled to Samaria, and "as far as Phoenicia, Cyprus and Antioch" (Acts 11:19).

The scattered believers preached the gospel wherever they went (Acts 8:4), and thus added many new converts to the faith. This created a need for follow-up, spiritual instruction, and encouragement for the new converts. For example, the apostles in Jerusalem sent Peter and John to Samaria to check out Philip's ministry (Acts 8:14), and they sent Barnabas to Antioch when they heard of Greeks being converted there (Acts 11:19-22).

Of course followers of Jesus, the Messiah, were already living in many foreign lands, having come to faith at Pentecost. Held fifty days after Passover, Pentecost (also called the Feast of Weeks) was a festival of thanksgiving for the harvested crops. Each year, Jews from many nations would gather in Jerusalem for this celebration. According to Acts 2:9-11 (NIV), "Parthians, Medes and Elamites; residents of Mesopotamia, Judea and Cappadocia, Pontus and Asia, Phrygia and Pamphylia, Egypt and the parts of Libya near Cyrene; visitors from Rome (both Jews and converts to Judaism); Cretans and Arabs" heard the Spirit-filled message in their native languages. They also heard Peter's powerful sermon (Acts 2:14-41), and many came to faith in Christ. Returning to their homes, these new converts became an international evangelistic team. In fact, it is likely that the church at Rome was established by those who had heard about Jesus and had believed in him in Jerusalem, at Pentecost.

James, as the leader of the Jerusalem Christian community and as shepherd to a scattered flock, wrote to this large group of Jewish believers in Christ who were living far beyond the walls of Jerusalem. Thus he addressed his letter, "To the twelve tribes scattered among the nations" (1:1 NIV). Because this letter was written early in the life of the church (before Paul's missionary journeys), nearly all of the believers would have been Jewish, but it is a book for all Christians, both Jewish and Gentile believers.

James knew what these young believers would be facing as they attempted to live for Christ, far away from the apostles and elders. There would be trials and persecutions, similar to what had driven many of them from their homes. There would be suffering. There would be temptations. There would be pressures. James was concerned that his Christian brothers and sisters should persevere.

James knew as well that it is easy to slip back into old habits or spiritual neutrality when one has moved away and is surrounded by those who believe differently. And so he challenged his readers to move beyond mere words into action—to live out their faith.

James was also concerned about the body, the fellowship, and the church. And so he warned of discrimination and divisions and urged believers to guard their speech, to seek divine wisdom, to be humble, and to pray for each other.

The first-century readers of this letter would have appreciated James's direct and practical approach. He got right to the point with Spirit-led answers that they needed.

MESSAGE

Living Faith, Trials, Law of Love, Wise Speech, and Wealth. These are the main topics covered in this letter. We will look closely at each one, considering its historical context, its meaning for first-century believers, and its application for today.

Because James was Christ's brother, it would have been natural for him to echo some of the predominant themes in Christ's teachings. And that is what you will find in this letter. In fact, the content of the book of James seems to follow closely what Jesus taught. Consider these similar passages (from the NIV):

- James (1:2): *Consider it pure joy, my brothers, whenever you face trials of many kinds.*

Jesus (Matthew 5:11-12): *Blessed are you when people insult you, persecute you and falsely say all kinds of evil against you because of me. Rejoice and be glad, because great is your reward in heaven, for in the same way they persecuted the prophets who were before you.*

■ James (2:12-13): *Speak and act as those who are going to be judged by the law that gives freedom, because judgment without mercy will be shown to anyone who has not been merciful. Mercy triumphs over judgment!*

Jesus (Matthew 6:14-15): *For if you forgive men when they sin against you, your heavenly Father will also forgive you. But if you do not forgive men their sins, your Father will not forgive your sins.*

■ James (3:11-13): *Can both fresh water and salt water flow from the same spring? My brothers, can a fig tree bear olives, or a grapevine bear figs? Neither can a salt spring produce fresh water. Who is wise and understanding among you? Let him show it by his good life, by deeds done in the humility that comes from wisdom.*

Jesus (Matthew 7:16-20): *By their fruit you will recognize them. Do people pick grapes from thornbushes, or figs from thistles? Likewise every good tree bears good fruit, but a bad tree bears bad fruit. A good tree cannot bear bad fruit, and a bad tree cannot bear good fruit. Every tree that does not bear good fruit is cut down and thrown into the fire. Thus, by their fruit you will recognize them.*

■ James (5:12): *Above all, my brothers, do not swear—not by heaven or by earth or by anything else. Let your "Yes" be yes, and your "No," no, or you will be condemned.*

Jesus (Matthew 5:34-37): *But I tell you, Do not swear at all: either by heaven, for it is God's throne; or by the earth, for it is his footstool; or by Jerusalem, for it is the city of the Great King. And do not swear by your head, for you cannot make even one hair white or black. Simply let your "Yes" be "Yes," and your "No," "No"; anything beyond this comes from the evil one.*

Echoing Jesus, James gave his scattered flock a practical handbook for Christian living in a hostile world.

Living Faith (1:19–2:26). This is the most familiar theme of the book and the most controversial. In fact, many have believed that what James wrote about "faith and works" contradicts the teachings of Paul. It is easy to see why. James wrote (according to the NIV):

- *Faith by itself, if it is not accompanied by action, is dead; faith without deeds is useless* (2:17-20).
- *Was not our ancestor Abraham considered righteous for what he did when he offered his son Isaac on the altar? You see that his faith and his actions were working together, and his faith was made complete by what he did. And the scripture was fulfilled that says, "Abraham believed God, and it was credited to him as righteousness," and he was called God's friend. You see that a person is justified by what he does and not by faith alone* (2:21-24).
- *As the body without the spirit is dead, so faith without deeds is dead* (2:26).

On the other hand, Paul wrote (according to the NIV):

- *For we maintain that a man is justified by faith apart from observing the law* (Romans 3:28).
- *If, in fact, Abraham was justified by works, he had something to boast about—but not before God. What does the Scripture say? "Abraham believed God, and it was credited to him as righteousness"* (Romans 4:2-3).
- *The only thing that counts is faith expressing itself through love* (Galatians 5:6).
- *For it is by grace you have been saved, through faith—and this not from yourselves, it is the gift of God—not by works, so that no one can boast* (Ephesians 2:8-9).

It sounds as though James is saying that we are justified (made righteous in God's sight) by what we do ("deeds" or "works"), where Paul is saying that we are justified by faith alone, not by works.

But there is really no contradiction. Here's why:

First, both James and Paul used the same working definition of "saving faith"—total trust in Jesus Christ. Consider these examples from James (NIV): "the testing of your faith develops perseverance" (1:3); "But when he asks, he must believe and not doubt" (1:6); "And the prayer offered in faith will make the sick person well" (5:15). The words "faith" and "believe" clearly refer to heartfelt and sincere trust.

Paul explained saving faith similarly when he wrote: "The only thing that counts is faith working through love" (Galatians 5:6 NRSV); "Yet he [Abraham] did not waver through unbelief regarding the promise of God, but was strengthened in his faith and gave glory to God, being fully persuaded that God had power to do what he had promised. This is why "it was credited to him as righteousness" (Romans 4:20-22 NIV). Notice the phrases "did not waver," "being fully persuaded," and "expressing itself through love." To Paul, saving faith was not mere intellectual assent to the facts of the gospel—it was deep and sincere trust in Christ.

Second, both James and Paul were writing to correct misunderstandings of the relationship between faith and works in the process of justification. But they were correcting different problems.

James wrote to correct "easy-believe-ism," the kind of superficial belief in Christ that is mere intellectual assent—the attitude that turns faith into cold orthodoxy, with the person merely believing the right facts about God and Jesus. James explained it this way: "You believe that there is one God. You do well. Even the demons believe—and tremble" (2:19 NKJV). Obviously, demons aren't Christians, and yet in one respect they are "believers." Their kind of belief is far from the faith that saves.

The Jerusalem church had experienced tremendous growth. With this growth there undoubtedly were many "hangers on," spiritual groupies, people who wanted to be part of the Christian crowd but had no depth to their faith. Ananias and Sapphira seem to fit into that category. Their phony profession and dramatic deaths rocked the young church (see Acts 5:1-11). Later in the New Testament, we hear of others who left churches when the going got tough: "They went out from us, but they did not belong to us; for if they had belonged to us, they would have remained with us. But by going out they made it plain that none of them belongs to us" (1 John 2:19 NRSV).

To deal with this problem head-on, under the inspiration of the Holy Spirit James pronounced that superficial faith, just believing the facts about Christ, is not enough. True faith involves wholehearted and genuine trust in Jesus Christ and will be evidenced by a changed life. In other words, true faith will produce good works.

Paul's statements, on the other hand, were meant to counter a Jewish emphasis on obeying the law (especially the ceremonial law as given in the Pentateuch). Many Jews who had come to faith in Christ felt obligated to observe Jewish laws and customs—some going so far as to insist that all new believers, even Gentiles, should keep Jewish laws, especially circumcision. Paul's strong teaching was that the purpose of the law was to prepare the way for the Messiah (making people aware of their sinfulness and providing a picture of God's perfect sacrifice for sin)—thus the law was fulfilled in Christ. Believers, therefore, were under no obligation to obey Jewish laws. Paul made it clear that salvation is *by grace through faith*, not by slavish obedience to the laws. Listen to what Paul wrote to the Galatians, who were struggling with this issue:

- *You foolish Galatians! Who has bewitched you? Before your very eyes Jesus Christ was clearly portrayed as crucified. I would like to learn just one thing from you: Did you receive the Spirit by observing the law, or by believing what you heard? Are you so foolish? After beginning with the Spirit, are you now trying to attain your goal by human effort? Have you suffered so much for nothing—if it really was for nothing? Does God give you his Spirit and work miracles among you because you observe the law, or because you believe what you heard? Consider Abraham: "He believed God, and it was credited to him as righteousness."* (Galatians 3:1-6 NIV)

In fact, it was just this issue that brought Paul to the church council of Jerusalem. There, after Paul presented his case, James spoke for the elders and declared that the Gentile believers were not obligated to keep the Jewish ceremonial laws (see Acts 15:12-29).

In all of this, Paul's main point was that a person could never be good enough to "earn" his or her salvation. And because everyone has sinned, all people fall into this lost category—all fall short. "This righteousness from God comes through faith in Jesus Christ to all who believe. There is no difference, for all have sinned and fall short of the glory of God, and are justified freely by his grace through the redemption that came by Christ Jesus" (Romans 3:22-24 NIV). Interestingly, James also underlined the universality of sin and the need for salvation when he wrote: "For whoever shall keep the whole law and yet stumbles in one point, he is guilty of all" (2:10 NKJV).

In summary, James was speaking of good deeds *after* conversion, as evidence of faith and a right relationship with God—true faith produces good works. Paul was speaking of good deeds *before* conversion—they can never earn or produce a right relationship with God—obedience *follows* profession.

Importance for Today. The problem faced by James in the first century is one that is prevalent today. Churches are filled with people who *claim* to be followers of Christ. Unfortunately, however, the claims of many of those professed followers are hollow because their faith is shallow—their lives belie their profession by specific non-Christian actions and attitudes or by what they fail to do. And consider the countless number of people who use Christ, Christianity, and the church for personal gain (for example, politicians who want votes, salespeople who want contacts, merchants who want customers, and even preachers who want money)—they have a Christianity of convenience. According to many polls, most Americans say that they are Christians, many of the "born again" variety. But these same pollsters have found that most Americans are also biblically illiterate. And considering the huge social needs in the country—poverty, homelessness, teenage pregnancy, substance abuse, racism, child abuse, divorce, etc.—it would be fair to ask, "If so many Americans are Christians, why do these problems exist? Why don't all these believers make a difference for Christ?"

James would answer that not all who claim to have faith in Christ actually do—some are followers in word only: "Do not merely listen to the word, and so deceive yourselves. Do what it says" (1:22 NIV); "What good is it, my brothers, if a man claims to have faith but has no deeds? . . . Faith by itself, if it is not accompanied by action, is dead" (2:14, 17 NIV); "Show me your faith without your works, and I will show you my faith by my works. You believe that there is one God. You do well. Even the demons believe—and tremble" (2:18-19 NKJV).

The application of this theme in the book of James is clear: the church must continually call people to genuine faith in Christ—faith that results in changed lives. And individual Christians should evaluate their level of obedience to their Master and recommit to doing the good works that result from being saved.

How deep is your faith? Do you merely know a lot about God, or do you really know him? Do you have a superficial faith, or do you have a deep trust?

Trials (1:2-18; 5:7-11). The early church was born at a time of severe trials—remember, James was writing to believers who had been scattered throughout the world by persecution. So it should come as no surprise to find that one of the major themes in this book is how to react to trials and testing.

Many of these trials came from the *outside*. Zealous Jews, like Saul of Tarsus before his conversion, imprisoned and killed followers of Christ (Acts 6:8–7:60) and chased them throughout the countryside (Acts 8:1-3; 9:1-2). And Herod arrested church members, executed John's brother, James, and meant to do the same to Peter (Acts 12:1-5). Also, it seems that many in the Jerusalem church were being taken to court by rich people (2:6-7) and oppressed by landlords (5:4-6). Public acknowledgment of Christ as Savior and Lord did not lead to popularity, power, and prestige.

James's straight and clear message was to *welcome* these trials because, "the testing of your faith develops perseverance. Perseverance must finish its work so that you may be mature and complete, not lacking anything. . . . Blessed is the man who perseveres under trial, because when he has stood the test, he will receive the crown of life that God has promised to those who love him" (1:3–4, 12 NIV). Believers should be patient, standing firm in the faith and looking for Christ's return (5:7–8).

James also knew of the struggles that would occur on the *inside*. A trial can test believers' faith, causing doubts and discouragement and making them susceptible to a variety of temptations. And Satan tries to use tough times to divide the church. So James challenged his young flock to recognize the sources of their problems—their sin nature and the evil one (1:13–16), to keep focused on God and his goodness (1:17–18), and to resist Satan's subtle attacks (4:7).

Importance for Today. Persecutions and trials still come to the followers of Christ. Although we don't have King Herod or Pharisees to worry about, there are many in our world who would persecute us for following Christ. The way of the cross is not the way of the world—our values, priorities, and life-style can be very threatening to those who don't know the Savior. A Christian may have to make a difficult decision at work that could cost a promotion or even the job. A student may lose popularity at school for saying no and going against the tide of peers. Every day, Christians face scores of decisions that could result in being "persecuted" for their faith.

In addition, adversity is a part of life, a result of being mortal and human. We live in a fallen world; and people, all people, get sick, struggle through life, and eventually die. God doesn't promise to spare us from those trials and give us perpetual health, wealth, and good feelings. But he does promise to be with us in everything we face (see John 16:31-33; Romans 8:35-39).

So today, James would urge us, like his first-century readers, to see our trials as tests of faith that can help us grow and mature (1:3–4, 12). He would also tell us, however, to distinguish between external trials and internal temptations, which are rooted in the sinful nature (1:13–15). These self-centered desires must be resisted, and we should focus on God and his love and truth and not on ourselves (1:16–18).

There is also a clear application for local churches. During difficult times, they should be on guard for Satan's attacks as he tries to cause division and strife. In a recession, for example, many church members may lose their jobs while others continue to flourish economically. This could cause resentment and even a feeling of economic stratification in a church. And personal struggles can become grist for the gossip mill. (No wonder James wrote so much about the tongue—more on this later.) Instead of allowing tough times to divide us, let us pray and work to face them together—with believers encouraging and helping one another.

How are you responding to the trials in your life? Are you giving in or keeping the faith? Are you allowing tough times to separate you from other Christians or pull you together?

Law of Love (1:27; 2:8-17; 3:17-18; 4:11-12; 5:19-20). We have already discussed how James wrote this epistle before the controversy about whether or not Christians needed to obey Jewish ceremonial laws. Therefore, James had little to say about the Old Testament laws as such. But he did tell those who were careful to keep every point of the law that they were "lawbreakers" themselves if they stumbled "at just one point" (2:9-10), and he warned them against judging others (4:11-12). It seems as though James may have been sensing the emergence of the law-versus-grace tension in the Christian community.

We also discussed how much of what James taught echoes the teachings of Jesus, his older brother. This is also evident in James's references to "the perfect law of liberty" (1:25; 2:12) and "the royal law" (2:8). Jesus' summary of the Old Testament laws was, "Love the Lord your God with all your heart and with all your soul and with all your mind" and "'Love your neighbor as yourself.' All the Law and the Prophets hang on these two commandments" (Matthew 22:37-40 NIV). He also said, "In everything do to others as you would have them do to you, for this is the law and the prophets" (Matthew 7:12 NRSV). This emphasis on "loving your neighbor" and "doing for others" was also known as the "royal law" or the "law of love" (see Leviticus 19:18).

For James, the law of love included looking after "orphans and widows" (1:27), not showing favoritism (2:8-9), being merciful (2:12-13), clothing the naked and feeding the hungry (2:14-17), being a peacemaker (3:17-18), not speaking evil of another (4:11-12), and praying for each other (5:13-16). In fact, keeping the royal law is a powerful demonstration of our faith in Christ, as we discussed earlier under "living faith."

Importance for Today. James would be the first to emphasize the importance of having piety and purity in the midst of a twisted and morally depraved society (1:21-27; 4:4)—and certainly our society fits that description. But we can be so obsessed with keeping our hands clean and being separate from the world that we fail to reach out to those in need.

Also, very often our giving is meager or self-centered. A response to the poor and needy might be seasonal (for example, canned food drives at Thanksgiving and toy collections at Christmas) or small, an occasional dollar dropped in a solicitor's container. And our financial donations can be tithes to ourselves: beautiful edifices for worship and Christian education, exciting programs and literature, articulate and dynamic pastors—all provided for us and our families.

Our world is filled with those who need compassion, mercy, and love translated into food, shelter, medical care, counsel, and friendship. God's message to the church, and thus to us, through James is to obey the law of love. This means supporting Christian welfare and mission agencies and individuals with our prayers and money. It also means being sensitive to the needs in our neighborhoods and looking for ways that we can become involved personally. "If you really fulfill the royal law according to the Scripture, 'You shall love your neighbor as yourself,' you do well" (2:8 NKJV).

Are you obeying the law of love? Are you holding tightly to your money, or are you giving to those in need? Are you focused on your own comfort, or are you sacrificing to help others?

Wise Speech (1:19, 26; 3:1-18; 4:11-16; 5:9, 12). James began his chapter on the tongue by referring to "teachers." In the Jewish community, teachers, especially rabbis who taught God's Word, were held in high regard. To become a teacher, a boy had to study for many years under learned men. Paul, for example, was taught by the esteemed Gamaliel (Acts 22:3; see also Acts 5:34). In the new community of Christians, however, the first authorities and teachers were the apostles (Acts 2:42) who taught daily in the temple courts and from house to house (Acts 5:42).

Soon the church became so large that the disciples had to appoint "deacons" to oversee the distribution of food to widows and other needy people among them. This would allow the apostles to concentrate on their teaching ministry (Acts 6:1-6). The men selected as deacons were "full of the Spirit and of wisdom" (Acts 6:3 NRSV). Eventually, the deacons also became teachers and evangelists (Acts 5:42; 8:4). Other men, like James, were appointed to leadership positions in the church (see Acts 13:1-3). Eventually Paul would explain spiritual gifts and how the gifts should be used to build up the body of Christ (see especially 1 Corinthians 12 and Ephesians 4).

At the time James wrote this book, however, it seems as though many wanted to be teachers in the church, even though they weren't qualified. It is in this context and to those who "presumed to be teachers" that James wrote his words about the tongue and godly wisdom.

James began by warning aspiring teachers that they would be judged very strictly (3:1-2). He then discussed the issue of speech. Of all people, teachers should watch what they say, since most of what they teach directly impacts others.

Next, James discussed "wisdom." Although this may seem to be an abrupt change of thought and a new topic, there is a definite connection between "wisdom," "speech," and teachers. The key to controlling the tongue is to rely on God's wisdom and insight, and not be led by envy and selfish ambition (3:13-17). In fact, the ability of a person to control his or her tongue tells much about that person's relationship with God. Teachers are known as "wise" people; after all, they have the answers, and they tell us what to do and teach us how to think. But true wisdom comes from God and will show up in a person's life (3:13), not just in his or her words.

James's readers learned that they would have to be wise and then use their tongues wisely if they ever wanted to become teachers.

Importance for Today. Today, almost any believer can have a teaching role in the church as pastor, elder, Sunday school teacher, youth sponsor, small group leader, counselor, or Bible study teacher. And even if they don't have a recognized teaching position in the church, mature Christians should teach and encourage new believers in the faith. To these teachers in our churches, James would say, "What is the source of your teaching? Where is the wisdom? Watch what you say and make sure it is from God."

Beyond the issue of teachers and teaching, there is a strong application to all believers to guard our mouths. It is easy to be critical of others, to get in the last word, to complain, to brag of our accomplishments, or just to talk to hear ourselves. But those words come directly from "envy and selfish ambition" (3:14). And nothing hurts churches or relationships more quickly than careless or harmful talk.

Instead, we should "be quick to listen, slow to speak" (1:19), keep a "tight rein" on our tongues (1:26), refrain from judging our neighbors (4:11-12), avoid bragging (4:16) and complaining (5:9), and speak truthfully (5:12). We need to engage our minds before we put our mouths in gear and ask God for self-control. True believers in Christ should be known for their wise speech.

How is your speech? Are you quick to defend yourself and to get in an authoritative word, or are you a good listener? Do you voice your grievances and blast your opponents, or do you try to speak constructively? Are you quick to pass on the morsel of gossip, or do you remain silent and think the best of others?

Wealth (1:9-12; 2:1-7; 5:1-6). It is not surprising that there are significant references in James's epistle to wealth, especially the relationship between the poor and the rich, because the church in Jerusalem was poor. In fact, this church eventually became so impoverished, especially after a devastating famine, that Paul collected money for them on his third missionary journey (see Acts 11:28-30; 24:17; Romans 15:25-26; 1 Corinthians 16:1-4; 2 Corinthians 8:1–9:5).

The Jerusalem church was never a wealthy church. Remember, many of the apostles had been fishermen, and most of the early members came from the poor and oppressed classes. Also, Jesus associated with tax collectors and sinners (Matthew 9:9-13). Certainly identifying with Christ did not lead to advancement in career or prestige in the community; the opposite was true—following Christ could mean losing employment, friendships, and even family. The church was not a gathering place for the rich and powerful.

Another factor that contributed to their poverty was the emphasis on caring for the needy and feeding the hungry in the church. In Acts we read about the concern for widows and the daily distribution of food (Acts 6:1-4). Providing food for so many must have been a drain on their personal financial resources. In addition, there were conflicts between the rich and the poor. In the text we read that the rich were exploiting the poor and taking them to court (2:6-7). As in most cultures, society was stratified according to wealth with many becoming rich at the expense of the poor (5:4-6).

It is easy to imagine the mixed feelings of poor Christians: from a human standpoint they envied the rich and wanted to curry their favor with the hope of moving out of poverty, or they may have been filled with anger and desired revenge. Yet as followers of Christ, they were to love their neighbors (2:8).

James's message was direct and clear to both the poor and the rich. To the poor, he gave words of hope, and to the rich, words of warning. First, the poor should realize that they had a "high position" even though they were at the bottom in society (1:9). Second, they should not fawn over wealthy people who came to the church meetings. Wealth was not a mark of spirituality (in fact, the opposite was usually the case), and showing favoritism is a sin (2:1-9). Third, the poor should remember that what really counts is being rich in God's sight—"the man who perseveres under trial . . . will receive the crown of life that God has promised to those who love him" (1:12 NIV).

James warned the rich that their powerful and comfortable position was temporary and would soon "pass away like a flower of the field" (1:10-11 NKJV). Their gold and silver would corrode and their expensive clothing would rot (5:2-3). And he told rich oppressors that they would be punished for hoarding wealth, cheating workers, and wiping out their opposition (5:1-6). The rich would be condemned not for having wealth, but for what they did to become wealthy and how they used their riches. In addition to oppressing the poor, these people were living in luxury and self-indulgence (5:5).

Importance for Today. Today, Western society is intensely materialistic. People are obsessed with being comfortable, amassing possessions, and becoming rich. The "good life" involves conspicuous consumption and self-indulgence. Preying on this lust for wealth are con artists and profiteers, offering get-rich-quick schemes to the gullible. Even the government promises easy wealth through state-sponsored gaming and lotteries. Although much has changed since the first century, society is still stratified, with the wealthy and powerful featured as heroes and role models. Many of the rich use their money to get their way and to oppress the poor. And whatever the source of the wealth, very little is given to help the needy—rather it is hoarded for the last days, for one's retirement funds or estate (5:3).

Unfortunately, the church often reflects its own culture. Most Western churches are not poor, like the Jerusalem church. Instead, they are rich by comparison. Additionally, many churches and media "evangelists" also seem to be focused on money, catering to the rich and urging generous contributions. God's values are turned upside down.

James's message hits home. People are foolish (both Christians and non-Christians) to spend their lives on money. Chasing wealth is a futile pursuit because in God's eyes money is worth so little in comparison with what is important and valuable in life—seeking his kingdom and righteousness (Matthew 6:33). God will supply all our needs (Philippians 4:19), so we should trust him and live as he says. Money *is* important, but God tells us not to worry about it, because he will take care of us. The main trap of accumulating wealth is that it can give a false sense of security; that is, we can begin to trust in money instead of God. Money is the way people get what they need in this world, but God owns it all—we should worship him, not the cash. We need to get our values straight.

James also reminds us in our churches that, like the "discriminating" members of the Jerusalem church, we sin when we favor the rich over the poor. Consider the treatment of the following visitors to a typical church on Sunday: a man "wearing a gold ring and fine clothes, and a poor man in shabby clothes" (2:2 NIV). How might the greeters react? What about the other members? James would remind us: "If you show partiality, you commit sin" (2:9 NKJV).

Another application of James's message is how we treat the poor in our communities and neighborhoods. Do we oppress? Do we help? Do we reach out with food, clothes, medicine, and love in the name of Christ? And what about how we use our "wealth"? Compared to the very wealthy, we may feel poor; but compared to the destitute, we are rich. Regardless of the amount of money we have, we are responsible for how we use it (Matthew 25:14-30). True believers should be known for their generosity. (See also Matthew 6:19-34; 25:31-46; 1 Timothy 6:10, 17-19.)

What role does money play in your life? Are you obsessed with gaining wealth, or do you see money as a resource to be used for good? Do you spend, spend, spend on yourself, or are you a good steward of the time, money, and other resources entrusted to you? Do you work to be popular with the rich and influential, or do you associate with the poor, regardless of what others may say or think?

VITAL STATISTICS

Purpose: To expose hypocritical practices and to teach right Christian behavior

Author: James, Jesus' brother, a leader in the Jerusalem church

To whom written: First-century Jewish Christians residing in Gentile communities outside Palestine, and to all Christians everywhere

Date written: Probably A.D. 49, prior to the Jerusalem council held in A.D. 50

Setting: This letter expresses James's concern for persecuted Christians who were once part of the Jerusalem church

Key verse: "But someone will say, 'You have faith; I have deeds.' Show me your faith without deeds, and I will show you my faith by what I do" (2:18).

OUTLINE

1. Genuine religion (1:1-27)
2. Genuine faith (2:1-3:12)
3. Genuine wisdom (3:13–5:20)

Modern names and boundaries are shown in gray

Mediterranean Sea

Aegean Sea

Cape Salmone

James addressed his letter "to the twelve tribes scattered among the nations" (1:1 NIV). After Stephen was martyred (Acts 7:55—8:2), persecution increased, and Christians in Jerusalem were scattered throughout the Roman world. There were thriving Jewish communities in Rome, Alexandria, Cyprus, and cities in Greece and Asia Minor.

Because these believers did not yet have the support of established Christian churches, James, as a concerned leader, wrote to encourage them in their faith during that difficult time.

James 1

GREETINGS / 1:1

How often do we open a letter without checking to see who sent it? Ancient letter writers signed their names right at the beginning, so readers immediately knew the source. Modern readers of the New Testament, however, frequently skip over the address. It strikes us as unimportant. Our oversight is a mistake. The first verses of New Testament books often tell us the writer's identity and how the writers perceived their roles. In James's case, these helpful insights prepare us for the entire letter. We treat letters with more respect when we understand who sent them and why.

THEMES IN JAMES 1

Chapter 1 of this letter functions like an overture to a great piece of music. Themes are introduced to which the writer will return later in the letter. There are four main themes in the first chapter.

1. Joyful living requires self-control and contentment. Even in trials, joy should be our chosen response. Joy allows us to endure the test until it has accomplished its purpose. So, contentment leads to self-control, which clears the way for further contentment. Understanding the purposes of trials and the importance of joy will require wisdom, which comes from God. Are you content?

2. Wisdom combines what we know with what we must do. God is our source of wisdom. He is willing to give complete wisdom to all those who ask him in faith. God's wisdom is not just a certain way of knowing or thinking. Like faith, it is practical and active. Have you asked for it?

3. Hypocrisy occurs whenever belief and action are separated. For the Christian, hypocrisy is unacceptable. God's wisdom leads us away from hypocrisy and toward a life of hearing and doing God's commands. Are you listening to and doing what God has said?

4. Christians must live their faith, not just talk about it. Real Christianity is ethics at the very core. Are you doing what you say you believe?

1:1 James. James is mentioned by name only a few times elsewhere in the New Testament (Matthew 13:53-55; Acts 1:12-14; 15:12-21; 1 Corinthians 15:3-8; Galatians 1:19; 2:7-9). But as the leader of the Jerusalem church, he was known on a first-name basis by the rapidly expanding Christian world. By simply using his first name, James manages to convey both humility and authority as he signs his letter.

He could have identified himself as "brother of Jesus" or "leader of the Jerusalem church," but the only addition to his name is the title of servant. Real authority doesn't need to promote itself. It was often said that Jesus spoke with unusual authority (Matthew 7:28-29; Mark 1:22, 27). The quality of Jesus' message had the ring of truth. James's name must have conveyed that same kind of authority. He felt no need to identify himself as Jesus' brother. It was not that role that gave James his authority anyway. His authority came from recognizing and confessing that Jesus, his brother, was also his Lord.

The effectiveness of our spiritual authority will always depend on the source of that authority. Religious education, titles, power, accomplishments, reputation, and self-image are short-lived and ineffective substitutes for a vital and obedient relationship with Jesus Christ. When we know Christ as Lord and obey him, we find his authority sufficient. He will be reflected in what we say and do.

> There is no city, no tribe, whether Greek or barbarian, in which Jewish law and Jewish customs have not taken root. *Josephus*

Servant of God. The Greek word *doulos* (slave, servant) refers to a position of complete obedience, utter humility, and unshakable loyalty. Obedience was the work, humility was the position, and loyalty was the relationship that a master expected from a slave. Many of the first followers of Christ were, in fact, slaves. But among Christians, the idea of being a slave of Christ became not a position of humiliation, but a place of honor. There can be no greater tribute to a believer than to be known as God's obedient, humble, and loyal servant. When we struggle to display any one of those qualities, we will tend to be weak in the others also. If Jesus actually is our Lord, our actions must be obedient to him, our attitude must be humble before him, and our life must be loyal to him.

Lord Jesus Christ. The three names that make up this title refer to the unique character of Jesus. He is the heavenly, exalted *Lord* who will one day return in glory to this world. He is *Jesus*, God come to earth as a human being. He is *Christ*, the anointed one who fulfilled God's purposes by dying for us.

JESUS AS LORD

The identification of Jesus Christ as Lord was a radical statement in James's time. To the Jews it was blasphemous because no human could be called "Lord," and to the Romans it was treason against the authority of the emperor. To everyone who claimed it, it was a sign of giving Christ control over life, career, and ultimate destiny. Thousands of believers eventually lost their lives in horrible ways because they would not take back their statement: "Jesus is Lord."

Today there are few places in the world where claiming Jesus as Lord is openly forbidden. This may be because the world has become a better place. But it is more likely that the world has simply discovered that today's believers don't quite mean it as seriously and completely when they say "Jesus is Lord" as the early believers did. Perhaps the biggest difference is that early Christians backed up what they said with their very lives, while today "Jesus is Lord" is merely a cliché, a slogan, or a bumper sticker. The unspoken question of the entire letter of James is: To what degree will you be a servant of God and the Lord Jesus Christ?

The twelve tribes. The original twelve tribes of Israel no longer existed. Deportation of the ten northern tribes had effectively destroyed their identity. All that was left of that part of Israel were the mixed-race Samaritans who were despised by the Jews. By the time of this letter the term *the twelve tribes* had come to describe the regathered and renewed Israel that God would create in the last days (Ezekiel 47:13; Matthew 19:28; Revelation 7:4-8; 21:12). That regathering has been made possible by Jesus the Messiah.

Scattered. [NRSV] The phrase "scattered among the nations" translates the Greek word *diaspora*, a technical term referring to Jews who had left Palestine by force or by choice. The deportation of Jews to foreign lands had been practiced since the days of the Assyrians over six hundred years before Christ. But many Jews had also emigrated to other lands in the quest for wealth and opportunity. This network of Jewish communities scattered throughout the Roman Empire became the stepping stone for the spread of the gospel. The book of Acts describes the missionary pattern of Paul and others. In almost every town they visited, the presence of a Jewish synagogue gave them an open forum from which to communicate the Good News. What history records as the splintering of the nation of Israel was used by God to facilitate the spread of his Word.

Following the resurrection of Christ and the early successes of the young church in Jerusalem, the believers were severely persecuted. They were forced to escape to distant places. Taking their faith with them, they began to carry out the commission Christ had given his disciples in Matthew 28:19: "Go therefore and make disciples of all the nations" (NKJV).

The sense of accountability to the church in Jerusalem remained strong until the destruction of the city in A.D. 70. Paul's missionary journeys included reports to the apostles there. Early conflicts within the church were discussed and settled in Jerusalem (Acts 15). This letter from James indicates that there may have been regular channels of communication between groups of believers.

Greetings. As if to acknowledge the foreign environment of the believers to whom he is writing, James uses a typical Greek expression for his greeting. The term he uses, *chairein*, conveys a sense of joy or happiness. James will not delay in moving to the pressing matters which have motivated his letter. This same greeting (Acts 15:23) is used in the first circular letter written to believers outside Jerusalem after the first special council, recorded in Acts 15. James helped write that letter also.

ENDURING TRIALS AND TEMPTATIONS / 1:2-18

James wrote to believers facing difficult times. Their troubles ranged from personal trials to disabling doubts; from persecution for following Christ to the lure of respectability in their community and the dangers of spiritual pride. James wrote to encourage his brothers and sisters in their faith.

James's approach illustrates the variety of forms that encouragement can take. At times, James confronts. In other places, he gently encourages. He uses hyperbole (extreme illustration) in a way that reminds us of his half brother, Jesus. Sparks and forest fires, rudders and large ships create mental pictures like Jesus created with his needles and camels. James even uses humor as a tool to encourage. He is clearly someone who practices the truth of Hebrews 10:24, "And let us consider how we may spur one another on toward love and good deeds" (NIV). He begins his letter looking directly at trials and daring to spur his fellow believers with a challenge: "Meet the very worst that life presents you with joy."

1:2 Consider it pure joy . . . whenever you face trials.[NIV] How can a person consider trials a reason for joy? This is a remarkable command—we are to choose to be joyful in situations where joy would naturally be our last response. When certain circumstances make us angry and we want to blame the Lord, James directs us to the healthier alternative—joy. When trials come, "don't resent them as intruders, but welcome them as friends" (Phillips). Those who trust in God ought to exhibit a dramatically different, positive response to the difficult events of life.

Our attitude is to be one of *pure joy* (genuine rejoicing). This is not joyful anticipation *for* trials. Instead, it is joy *during* trials. The joy is based on confidence in the outcome of the trial. It is the startling realization that trials represent the possibility of growth. In contrast, most people are happy when they escape trials. But James encourages us to consider it pure joy in the very face of trials. The response he is describing may include a variety of feelings, but it is not simply based on emotions. James is not encouraging believers to pretend to be happy. Rejoicing goes beyond happiness. Happiness centers on earthly circumstances and how well things are going here. Joy is God-oriented rather than event-oriented because it centers on God and his presence in our experience.

JOY
Joy is a deep sense of well-being that may at the same time embrace sorrow, tears, laughter, anger, pain. Joy is more a decision than a feeling. It is choosing to live above feelings but not deny them. It is not intense happiness, although choosing joy sometimes produces happiness. Joy is a particularly Christian response to life since it depends on faith in God's sovereignty. It is quiet and grateful, and it inwardly delights in the goodness of God. Joy can be understood in the context of the two other main responses to life:
1. *Drifting.* Some float in the ebb and flow of life's experiences, hoping one moment and despairing the next. This response leaves the person entirely at the mercy of the events of life.
2. *Pretending.* Some pretend to be happy, determined to put up a good front, no matter what the circumstances. In comparison with these two, joy is more honest. It admits to hurts. It recognizes suffering and willingly participates in it. Joy is a contentment that comes from realizing that nothing can "separate us from the love of God that is in Christ Jesus our Lord" (Romans 8:39).

Consider means "chalk it up," or "regard it as." Count it pure joy because your experience of trial is evidence that you will grow. Don't let pain or struggle take away the joy of new growth, new insight, new depth, or new dependency. Focus on the future benefits of your difficult time.

My brothers. By using this term repeatedly, James emphasizes Christian solidarity with all who read his letter. It reminds us that the lessons in this book are for us. We rarely have to face trials alone. Believers always have Christ with them; they also have one another. When we attempt to manage pain, loneliness, failure, and other trials alone, we are not using the resources that God has made available through other believers. We are here to help each other. We are not to go it alone!

Whenever you face trials. *Whenever* doesn't allow much room for doubt. We are urged to be joyful not *if* we face trials, but *whenever*. To *face* trials is more literally expressed as to "fall into" trials. These are the unavoidable difficulties of life. Falling into trials is like falling among robbers, as did the traveler in Luke 10:30. Trials, problems, situations can be joy-robbers if we lack the proper attitude. Later in the chapter (1:13-15), James deals more directly with temptations that are self-inflicted. But there will be times when, no matter where we turn, we encounter trials.

Trials of many kinds. Where do these trials come from? They can be hardships from without or temptations from within. They come when we are least prepared and when we are most certain they could never come. A trial may be a hard situation that tests a person's faith such as persecution, a difficult moral choice, or a tragedy. Life's trail is marked with such trials. Enduring one trial is not enough. God's purpose in allowing this process is to develop complete maturity in us.

Considering your trials to be joy comes from seeing life with God's perspective in mind. We may not be able to understand the specific reasons for God's allowing certain experiences to crush us or wear us down, but we can be confident that his plan is for our good. What may look hopeless or impossible to us never looks that way to God!

1:3 **The testing of your faith produces endurance.** NRSV *Dokimion* is the Greek word translated *testing*; it means "approved after testing." Although we tend to think of testing as a way to prove what we don't know or don't have, testing ought to be seen as a positive opportunity to prove what we have learned. *Testing* is an important term because it is positive rather than negative. This is the exact term used in 1 Peter 1:6-7 for "proved genuine" and means that the trial is God's attempt to prove our faith genuine. It is a test that has a positive purpose. The person being tested should become stronger and purer through the testing. In this case, the trials do not determine whether or not believers have faith; rather, the trials strengthen believers by adding perseverance to the faith that is already present.

Endurance is faith stretched out; it involves trusting God for a long duration. In the context of the rest of the New Testament, it is important to see that James is not questioning the faith of his readers—he assumes that they trust in Christ. He is not convincing people to believe; he is encouraging believers to remain faithful to the end. James knows that their faith is real, but it lacks maturity.

We cannot really know our own depth until we see how we react under pressure. Diamonds are coal, subjected to intense pressure over a period of time. Without pressure, coal remains coal. The testing of your faith is the combined pressure that life brings to bear on you. Perseverance is the intended outcome of this testing. Other words that could be used for this outcome include "endurance," "steadfastness," "fortitude," and "staying power." The word *endurance* has a particular connection with this diamondlike quality created by testing, since the Latin root of this word means "to harden." Perseverance is not a passive submission to circumstances—it is a strong and active response to the difficult events of life. It is not passive endurance, but the quality of standing on your feet as you face the storms. It is not simply the attitude of withstanding trials, but the ability to turn them into glory, to overcome them.

THE PRACTICE FIELD OF FAITH

It is not just being tested that is good for us but passing the test. The testing is not just to see if you made the team, but to prepare you for higher service. It is like being proven in practice so you will be prepared for tougher competition.

Produces. This word was commonly used in agriculture to indicate the harvest or yield. Testing of faith produces a harvest, or the final product, perseverance. The results are gradual. There is an end in sight, but arriving there takes time.

When the writer of Hebrews portrayed the heroes of faith (Hebrews 11), the outstanding characteristic of the Old Testament men and women of faith was their endurance. They lived on a promise. They acted in faith. "Yet all these, though they were commended for their faith, did not receive what was promised" (Hebrews 11:39 NRSV). They stayed true to God even when they faced one of the most difficult hardships of all—not seeing the fulfillment of what had been promised to them. Elsewhere in the New Testament, perseverance is also noted as one of the essential parts of the believer's life (see Romans 2:7; 5:3-5; 8:24-25; 2 Corinthians 6:3-7; 2 Peter 1:2-9).

What makes trials so difficult to endure? It is not our nature to endure. When it comes to trials, we would rather escape, explain, or exit the difficulty. In fact, we will tend to do almost anything to avoid enduring a trial.

REACTIONS TO TRIALS

■ *Escape*—Our first line of defense is to avoid, deny, or escape. We don't want to face trials; we would sooner keep our back to them. But James is not writing here about avoidable trials. These are not difficulties to look for so we can practice endurance. These are trials and temptations that come looking for us.

Escape is certainly a valid strategy when it comes to those temptations and trials that we willfully walk right into by our habits or wrong choices. These are temptations that Paul urges us to "flee from" (1 Corinthians 6:18; 1 Timothy 6:3-11). The list includes envy, strife, malicious talk, evil suspicions, and sexual immorality. Peter reminds us that the problems caused by our disobedience need to be handled differently: "But how is it to your credit if you receive a beating for doing wrong and endure it? But if you suffer for doing good and you endure it, this is commendable before God" (1 Peter 2:20).

James gives us a plan for the worst-case scenario. It is James's answer to one of our questions: "When we are following Christ and find ourselves facing trials of many kinds, what do we do when there seems no way to escape?"

■ *Explain*—When we face trials, we tend to ask, "Why is this happening to me?" If only we could understand God's reasons, it would be much easier to endure whatever we are suffering. If we can explain, we can endure. But insisting on specific answers actually weakens our endurance. James does not encourage us to expect understanding. He urges us to get on with our service with joyful endurance, rather than attempt to explain every event that God allows into our life. What do we do when we face trials of many kinds and cannot explain them?

■ *Exit*—Once a trial is upon us, we want to get beyond it as quickly as possible. Any shortcut offered is tempting. But quick solutions to trials often involve compromise in areas that we should not negotiate. The temptation to revert to an old pattern, or indulge a habit, has not been joyfully endured if our resistance has only lasted a few minutes. Trials should not be allowed to outlast us; we are to outlast trials. Unfortunately, we are very much like the people who claim they are serious about training for long-distance races, but only succeed in running around the block once. A taste of hardship is no trial.

Even the commanded response of joy in trials will disappoint us if we expect that joy will eliminate the need for endurance. Our joy must itself develop endurance. At this point, our best example is Jesus, "who for the joy set before him endured the cross, scorning its shame, and sat down at the right hand of the throne of God" (Hebrews 12:2 NIV). James does not hesitate to encourage us in joyful endurance when our question is "What do we do when we face trials and there is no quick exit?"

1:4 Let endurance have its full effect.NRSV The word *perseverance* in Greek (*hupomone*) suggests "steadfastness under trial." What faithful perseverance generates is a whole person, recognized by three significant characteristics:

> By the way in which we meet every experience in life we are either fitting or unfitting ourselves for the task which God meant us to do.   *William Barclay*

1. **Mature**NRSV—seasoned, experienced, well-developed, fit for the tasks God sent us into the world to do. Maturity in this sense is not related to age. It is a quality developed by how much we have learned from the trials we have experienced. Someone has defined *experience* as the ability to recognize a mistake when we make it again. Maturity is the ability to recognize a mistake before we make it again. It is a trained ability to learn from each previous experience. But maturity takes time.

2. **Complete**—fully trained. The weaknesses and imperfections are being removed from our character; we are gaining victory over old sins; we are demonstrating a sense of competence about life. This completeness relates to the breadth of our experience. We have passed through **trials of many kinds.** To be complete means that we have become mature in many areas of life. God does not want cheap substitutes, but thoroughly developed Christians.

3. **Not lacking anything**NIV—the basic life skills are there, ready to be used; the obvious weaknesses or blind spots of the past have been corrected; more and more clearly we mirror Christ himself! We will not be lacking anything when we are mature

and complete in all the essential areas of life. Although this last quality is stated in the negative, it describes a security or contentment that comes from knowing that God has what we need, when we need it. Believing in God's faithfulness, we have everything we need.

TESTED FAITH IS STRONG FAITH

Tested faith brings about a depth of character	Romans 5:3-5
Tested faith enables us to comfort and encourage others	Corinthians 1:3-5
Tested faith increases dependence on God for wisdom	James 1:5; 3:17-18
Tested faith encourages us to lead a productive and effective life	2 Peter 1:5-9
Tested faith helps us to identify with Christ	Matthew 4:1-11 Hebrews 5:7-10
Tested faith allows us to focus on our future hope in Christ	Romans 8:18-24

Scripture does not promise us perfection in this life. So to be mature and complete is not sinless perfection. These terms describe a person who is fully committed to obeying God's commands. Perfection, as the Bible defines it for believers, is a right relationship with God expressed in a life of obedience. The work of perseverance is never done in this life, but there must be substantial progress. The writer of Hebrews is insistent: "Therefore let us leave the elementary teachings about Christ and go on to maturity, not laying again the foundation of repentance from acts that lead to death, and of faith in God" (Hebrews 6:1 NIV).

Where there is testing, there are failures along the way. It is possible to experience trials and *not* learn from them or develop perseverance. Growth is not guaranteed. But James fully expects believers to respond to trials with joy because they understand that the process is producing a deeper, more certain faith. He would expect no less from us.

1:5 If James 1:2-4 describes the benefits of responding correctly to trials, this verse draws attention to our hopelessness without

God's assistance, and how we can receive wisdom to triumph over trials. The shift is sudden and helpful. The command to consider (1:2) relates to the need for wisdom (1:5). We need a certain kind of wisdom in order to consider it pure joy when facing all kinds of difficulties. If we are paying attention to the implications of the first verses in this letter we will be struck with our lack of wisdom. That wisdom, says James, comes from God.

If any of you lacks wisdom. ^{NKJV} The wisdom that we need has three distinct characteristics:

1. *It is practical*—The wisdom from God relates to life even during the most trying times. It is not a wisdom isolated from suffering and trials. This wisdom is the tool by which trials are overcome. An intelligent person may have profound ideas, but a wise person puts profound ideas into action. Intelligence will allow someone to describe several reasons why the car broke down. The wise person chooses the most likely reason and proceeds to take action.

2. *It is divine*—God's wisdom goes beyond common sense. Common sense does not lead us to choose joy in the middle of trials. This wisdom begins with respect for God, leads to living by God's direction, and results in the ability to tell right from wrong. It is a wisdom that James will describe at length in chapter 3.

3. *It is Christlike*—Asking for wisdom is ultimately asking to be like Christ. The Bible identifies Christ as the "wisdom of God" (1 Corinthians 1:24; 2:1-7).

Ask God. Recognizing our lack of wisdom might cause us to despair, but God wants us to turn to him instead. How do we know that God has answered our request for wisdom? When trials come we will find ourselves responding with an attitude of joy. We will realize that joy is not our own doing, but is a gift.

Who gives generously to all. ^{NIV} Our request to God for wisdom ought to be shaped by the following qualities of God's giving:

■ *God gives generously.* Since God's generosity has included the gift of his own Son, "how will he not also, along with him, graciously give us all things?" (Romans 8:32 NIV). The wisdom we need is one of those "things" God will graciously give to us. The Greek expression in this verse could be translated "the giving God." God's generosity is universal. It is one of those basic characteristics of God that is revealed in creation. Jesus went further and guaranteed God's generosity to his children

(Matthew 7:7-11; Mark 11:24; Luke 11:9-13; John 15:7). What better request can we present to God than to take him at his word and ask for wisdom to face the inevitable trials?

- *God gives without strings attached.* God gives **ungrudgingly.**^{NRSV} God is not resentful of our dependence on him, but welcomes our requests. God does not complain or criticize us for our incompetence, nor is his help halfhearted. Because God does not reproach us, we can be honest with God in our prayers and pour out our deepest feelings to him. God accepts us and understands our weaknesses, so we can come to him when we face difficulties and suffering. So we must never hesitate but come boldly to God to get his wisdom.

It will be given to him.^{NKJV} God's reply is sure. The *it* here is wisdom. Note that what God promises is to supply the wisdom for what must be done. Decisions still will have to be made, and actions will have to be taken. The wisdom is God's guidance, not his removal of our participation. Following our prayer and God's answer, we will be back where we started, only better equipped to "consider it pure joy" (1:2).

We must remember that God's promises do not submit to our plans. This verse is not permitting us to ask God for wisdom to bring about our will. Instead, we should humbly ask him for wisdom to remain in his will.

1:6 Let him ask in faith.^{NKJV} The one condition for receiving this gift of God is *faith*. God will generously give wisdom, but the one who asks will not receive it if he does not have confidence that God will answer the request.

Our faith is being tested by various trials (1:2-4). That same faith must be directed toward God as we realize our need for his wisdom. When we ask, we *must believe*. Faith is single-minded commitment, trusting fully in God. Faith holds on to God during testing (see also Job 13:15; Daniel 3:16-18). It is continued confidence in God despite outward circumstances. The writer of Hebrews expresses both the importance of faith and the kind of faith that God requires: "And without faith it is impossible to please God, for whoever would approach him must believe that he exists and that he rewards those who seek him" (Hebrews 11:6 NRSV).

With no doubting.^{NKJV} *Doubt* means "a divided mind." Doubting here has nothing to do with doubting whether God can do something; rather, it describes a people "divided" between being self-centered and being God-centered. This is the reason why James adds the idea of the "wave," because it really means to be tossed to and fro between self and God. Doubting is trusting self more than God and being earth-centered rather than heaven-centered in our prayer requests and in handling the problems of this life.

WHAT DOES *AND NOT DOUBT* MEAN?
The phrase "without doubting" is not connected with new faith or weak faith or faltering faith. If it was, none of us would have our prayers answered. It is not honest intellectual doubt or lack of clarity about the solution. It is not confusion over whether it is right to ask. It *is* divided loyalty. It is doubting that God cares, that he is powerful, that he is good.

He who doubts is like a wave of the sea driven and tossed by the wind. NKJV The behavior of sea waves is unsettled, going back and forth, driven by the varying winds, like the doubter's mind. Such a person wavers between choices and may, in the end, make no decision at all. Circumstances become the decision makers in that person's life. When God's promises and commands are given equal authority with our feelings, desires, and the world's ideas, the result is an unsettled sea of indecision and chaos.

STRENGTH FOR A WAVERING HEART
How decisive are we when it comes to depending on God? To stabilize our wavering or doubtful mind, we must commit ourselves wholeheartedly to God. This means we must consider his advice and take it in every important detail of our life. If we want to stop being tossed about by our doubts, we should rely on God to show us what is best for us. To help us he has given us his Word, his Holy Spirit, and mature Christian companions. We can ask him for wisdom and trust that he will give it to us. Then our decisions will be sure and solid.

1:7 **That man should not think he will receive anything from the Lord.** NIV God's promises are not lottery tickets to be claimed in faint hopes that they will deliver what they describe. God's answers are not subject to the laws of probability and chance. God will do what he says he will do. He requires our trust. God's dependability is part of his character.

The person who asks trustingly does not determine how God will answer, but he or she can be confident in knowing that God will answer. The person who asks doubtfully has no right to expect anything. His or her request was not genuine. When it seems as if God hasn't answered our prayers, we need to begin the search for a solution by asking ourselves whether we were trusting when we prayed. If our loyalties are straightened out, God's answers to prayer are restored to us.

CAN GOD REALLY DO IT?
We can never remove the last shred of doubt. The father who came to Jesus' disciples, asking them to heal his boy (Mark 9:14-29), then said to Jesus, "if you are able to do anything, have pity on us and help us" (NRSV). Although this man felt the inadequacy of his faith, he was asking for help. God promises to give wisdom to those who ask for it. Instead of trying to rid yourself of all doubt, focus instead on wholehearted commitment to God (Deuteronomy 6:5; Psalm 119:2; Matthew 22:37).

1:8 He is a double-minded man, unstable. NKJV To be double-minded and unstable is to "trust" God and claim to be a believer and yet be filled with doubt, keeping other options open in case God does not prove to be dependable. A double-minded person is trying to be allied to both sides in a war. That person is a walking contradiction. Augustine confessed to this kind of thinking when he remembered one of his earliest prayers, "O Lord, grant me purity, but not yet!"

In all his ways. NKJV Instability is revealed not only in individuals' prayers, but in all they do. Our prayers reveal our view of God. But they also reveal our view of life. Life is made up of different areas—physical, mental, social, and spiritual—but it cannot be lived that way. Living comes at us as a whole. When indecisiveness marks our relationship with God, that instability will affect all of life.

The choice James presents us in verses 2-8 is clear:

- We can live a single-minded life of trust in God where every experience, including the trials we fall into, is another step in the process of becoming mature and complete persons. The single-minded person will still be capable of doubt. In fact, doubts may be some of the trials that person faces. These doubts fall into the category of the man who wisely confessed when he stood before Jesus, "I believe; help my unbelief!" (Mark 9:24 NKJV). Single-minded persons do not dwell on whether they can find a shred of doubt in themselves; rather, they concentrate on wholehearted commitment to God.

- We can live a double-minded life where every experience will be approached with doubt and lack of trust in God. The double-minded person doubts and refuses to stop doubting.

We must ask God for wisdom to keep making the right choice.

ARE YOU DOUBLE-MINDED?
- *Personal life*—Do you proclaim that physical exercise is a good, healthy, essential habit while refusing to participate?
- *Business life*—Do you loudly lobby for fair and ethical treatment for yourself while denying that same treatment to others?
- *Social life*—Are you two-faced among different groups of friends?
- *Spiritual life*—Are you attempting to serve God while compromising with the world's standards?

1:9 Next James turns his attention to potential differences among Christians—notably between rich and poor. Although they share a common bond in Christ, they will face different trials as their faith is tested. James returns to this theme throughout his letter.

The brother.[NIV] The trials that James has mentioned previously have no respect for status or wealth. Suffering is the great leveler of people. Even though the world may apply different standards, in Christ we speak of each other as brothers and sisters.

Some of the believers are **in humble circumstances.**[NIV] They are low on the socioeconomic scale. The Greek word here, *tapeinos*, means "insignificant in the world's eyes, lowly, relatively poor and powerless, lacking in material possessions." They receive the subtle honor of being mentioned first.

These scattered Jewish Christians, especially those in Palestine and Syria, would have been in such circumstances. They would have been ostracized by the Jews and were often disowned by their families. This was also a time of famine, and Christians may have suffered severely (Acts 11:28-29).

Take pride in his high position.[NIV] This *pride* is not an arrogance, but a rejoicing in the fact that, contrary to the world's opinion, God's opinion of them gives them great worth. The word is *kauchastho* (boast). It is used in this identical form four times in Jeremiah 9:23-24 in the Greek Old Testament (the Septuagint): "This is what the Lord says: 'Let not the wise man boast of his wisdom or the strong man boast of his strength or the rich man boast of his riches, but let him who boasts boast about this: that he understands and knows me, that I am the Lord, who exercises kindness, justice and righteousness on earth, for in these I delight,' declares the Lord'' (NIV) The only thing worth boasting about in this world is knowing God. And anyone who truly knows God will "boast" with humility.

The *high position* is a present reality for these believers. It is their rich heritage as children of God who live in anticipation of participating in Christ's eternal kingdom (2:5). They may be facing trials and persecution now, but they can take pride in the high position they have been given as God's very own children. The world may say that Christ's followers lack almost everything, but through the testing of their faith these believers will eventually demonstrate to the world that they actually are "not lacking anything" (1:4).

DIGNITY
Christianity brings a new dignity to the poor and not-so-influential people of this world. That dignity is most apparent in the church, where there are not (or should not be) any class distinctions. All believers share the distinction and dignity of being changed by the gospel and being charged with the mission of taking that same Good News to the rest of the world. Believers know they have dignity before God because Christ died for them. Mary, the mother of Jesus, is a great example of this truth. The dignity that she displayed when she realized what God had done for her is seen in her prayer of praise, called the *Magnificat* (Luke 1:46-55).

1:10 The rich. NRSV Since James does not specifically add the word *brother* to *rich*, and since he later has some words for the rich in general, some have concluded James must have been contrasting poor believers with rich unbelievers. But there are two significant reasons for concluding that both rich and poor here are believers. First, it is awkward to read this as a warning to unbelievers in an opening chapter encouraging those who are in God's family. Second, if James expected rich unbelievers to read his letter, his message would be even more confrontive. Certainly a rich person should recognize his mortality, but much more important is his repentance and belief in Christ.

Jesus used an unforgettable illustration to point out the difficulty rich people encounter in entering the kingdom of heaven (Matthew 19:23-26; Mark 10:23-27; Luke 18:24-27). No wonder the disciples were incredulous as they pictured a camel trying to squeeze through the eye of a needle. But Jesus identified the problem as being in the human will, not in God's willingness or

Whatever our social or economic situation, James challenges us to see beyond it to our eternal advantages. What we can have in Jesus Christ outweighs anything in this life. Knowing him gives us our high position, where we find our true dignity.

ability to save: "Jesus replied, 'What is impossible with men is possible with God'" (Luke 18:27 NIV).

As the gospel spread around the Mediterranean world, some who believed would have been rich Jews. Some, like Lydia in Philippi (Acts 16:11-15), were Gentiles, and wealthy. To such people, James gives a special challenge. He reminds them not to measure their worth by their riches nor to depend on their possessions for security and joy because earthly treasures will not last. Rich Christians need God's perspective on wealth so that they will use it humbly and productively for God's kingdom.

Should take pride in his low position. NIV Christians, rich and poor alike, were being persecuted for their faith. Wealth was not always an effective protection against mob violence (see Acts 17:1-9). As they were being persecuted, the rich looked very much like those who were poor, and certainly they were on the same level. This identification with poor believers could be part of the low position that James is pointing out. But, since wealth and poverty are realities both in and out of persecution, the challenge here must include a way for rich believers to view themselves.

The *low position* also means to be brought lower in Christ. That is, the rich are great in this world but are made equal to the poor in God's world. James 2:5 says that the poor are rich in faith. So James 1:9-11 means that while the poor are low in this world, they are high in God's eyes, and while the rich are high in this world, they are brought lower in God's eyes, and both can teach each other.

What is involved in their low position? They should take pride (healthy self-esteem) because:

- They no longer need the riches of this life as a basis for security.

- They have been accepted by Christ.

- They have also been given the privilege of identifying with Christ in suffering along with other believers (Philippians 3:10).

- Their chosen humility for the present will be rewarded in eternity (Matthew 23:12).

Wealth and the abilities that lead to wealth can create a barrier between us and God. If we are rich, or even if we live what we modestly call a "comfortable" lifestyle, James reminds us that our only lasting security is in a relationship with Christ. We must not trust what money and power seem to guarantee; instead, we must humbly trust in God and his eternal riches.

The NRSV captures the play on words in the parallel of *tapeinos/ tapeinosei* (lowly/lowliness) in the descriptions of the two believers, "Let the believer who is lowly boast in being raised up, and the rich in being brought low" (James 1:9-10).

As a flower of the field he will pass away. NKJV This phrase echoes Isaiah 40:6-8. We resist thoughts of death. James warns that this resistance is a significant danger for those who are rich. Wealth brings false security. In the desert, a rain shower will cause the grasses and flowers to sprout almost instantly, but as soon as the scorching sun hits them, they wither and die. The abundant comfort and security of one moment is gone the next.

WHAT DO YOU TRUST?
Suffering reminds us all that we are human and will also pass away. Wealth may offer temporary protection, but death cannot be bought off. Because believers trust God and not wealth for their security, they are free to use wealth in God's service. If your grip on this life's treasure is very tight, you may be ignoring what God says about your mortality.

1:11 **The sun rises with its scorching heat and withers the field.** NRSV James describes a common occurrence in the Middle East. Morning is often welcomed by colorful desert flowers, bursting from the cool night. Their death is sudden in the sun's *scorching heat.* This term can also refer to a sirocco, a hot southeast wind that blows straight off the desert like the wave of heat as an oven is opened (see Hosea 13:15).

The rich man also will fade away. NKJV This fading or withering is as sudden and unexpected as the death of the wildflowers. Death always intrudes. The frequent announcements of the death of well-known people are often made in shocked tones. Somehow, death is not supposed to happen to successful people. But it does. In fact, says James, a rich person can fade away **even while he goes about his business.** NIV Life is uncertain. Disaster is possible at any moment. The word translated *business (poreiais)* literally means "goings." Death interrupts our schedule, our busyness, our best-laid plans. It is foolish to trust in what will not last. The psalmist gives us an appropriate prayer: "Teach us to count our days, that we may gain a wise heart" (Psalm 90:12 NRSV). Whether the number of our days turns out to be large or small, each should be lived to the glory of God.

The poor should be glad that riches mean nothing to God; otherwise poor people would be considered unworthy. The rich should be glad that wealth means nothing to God, because wealth is easily lost. We find true wealth by developing our spiritual life, not financial assets. Stewardship will not happen until wealth is seen in its proper place. The rich young ruler (Matthew 19:16-24; Mark 10:17-22; Luke 18:18-30) could not follow the Lord because his wealth got in the way. He had to be willing to forsake that god before he could honestly consider the true God.

James begins his letter by making sure that believers, both poor and rich, see themselves in the same light before God (see Galatians 3:28; Colossians 3:11). James calls his readers to find hope in God's eternal promises.

1:12 Blessed. This Greek word, *makarios*, in common usage described the happiness of a carefree life. The Bible deepens the meaning of *blessed* to include a deep joy that comes from receiving God's favor. Jesus used this word in each of what are called the Beatitudes (Matthew 5:3-12). In that message, it is surprising to see the kind of people Jesus called "blessed." Using the lessons from James 1:2-4, we might find it helpful to express the Beatitudes in this pattern:

- The poor in spirit ought to consider it pure joy, for theirs is the kingdom of heaven.

- Those who mourn ought to consider it pure joy, for they will be comforted.

- Those who are meek ought to consider it pure joy, for they will inherit the earth.

- Those who hunger and thirst for righteousness ought to consider it pure joy, for they will be filled. And so on.

While James did not directly quote Jesus' words, many of James's expressions remind a reader of Christ's way of speaking. The content of this letter sounds very much like the Sermon on the Mount. When we are strongly influenced by someone else, we might unconsciously imitate that person's mannerisms and ways of speech. How often do people note that we speak about the same matters with the same care that Jesus expressed?

Joy-filled, then, **is the man who perseveres under trial.**[NIV] As athletes persevere in training in order to improve their abilities and endurance for competition, so Christians persevere in spiritual training, enduring the trials that will bring maturity and completeness. Today's trials will seem like training when we face tomorrow's challenges. The way to get into God's winner's circle is to love him and stay faithful even under pressure. James does not exhort us to enjoy pain or even claim that our trials are fun; rather, he tells us that the trials can serve a purpose—to prove and improve our faith and to give us an attitude of joy.

Such a one has stood the test. NRSV There is a finish line. There are successes along the way—spiritual progress has its mile markers. But the trials of this life are contained in this life. Someday the test will be over. Only then will we appreciate just how much we have needed these gifts:

- Faith in Christ
- Joy in the Lord
- Endurance under pressure
- Opportunities to pray confidently
- Wisdom from God
- Hope in a God who loves and values us

The phrase *stood the test* translates a Greek expression that literally means "having become approved." In the end, what matters is not whether our testing has been very difficult or very easy, but whether we have become approved through the tests. Near the end of his ministry, Paul used similar imagery as he summed up his life, "I have fought the good fight, I have finished the race, I have kept the faith. Now there is in store for me the crown of righteousness, which the Lord, the righteous Judge, will award to me on that day—and not only to me, but also to all who have longed for his appearing" (2 Timothy 4:7-8 NIV). James's words speak against the emphasis on instant results. The goals that he has mentioned so far—faith, endurance, maturity, perfection—all sound wonderful if we could only have them immediately. Instead we are faced with the race of life. God offers to help us along the way. What he chooses *not* to tell us is how long our personal race will be, nor what obstacles we will meet. We are directed to run with finishing on our minds, whatever it takes. Our dependence on God must be constant.

Will receive the crown of life. The first chapter of James teaches us that God's long-term goal for us is maturity and completeness, but his eternal goal for us is the crown of life. James used *crown of life* as the victory wreath from a Greek game, but the more essential idea is the Jewish idea of sovereignty and royalty.

The Greek term, *stephanon tes zoes* (the crown of life), is a rich expression of hope. The believer who endures trials by trusting God will have a life that, though not full of glory and honor, is still truly abundant, joyful, and victorious. Standing the tests of life gives believers even now a taste of eternity. But the struggles also lead to eternal life—the promise of glory in God's presence forever (see Revelation 2:10). We do not compete against each other, but against our own sins and against the course laid out for us (see Hebrews 12:1-2). So all who finish the race by keeping their faith in the face of suffering and temptation will be declared winners. Looking forward to that wonderful reward, and to the one who will present it to us, can be a source of strength and encouragement in times of trial (see also 1 Corinthians 9:24-27; 2 Timothy 4:7-8).

RUN TO FINISH

The sport of cross-country racing presents an athlete with unusual challenges. Each competitor must run against the clock over a course that may include hills, valleys, and mud. Wind and rain may add to their difficulties. Sometimes just finding the path is difficult. The three-mile race is a grueling test of endurance. Runners end the race filthy and exhausted. Often the group that crosses the finish line is much smaller than the group that began the race.

Each cross-country athlete is also part of a team. During the race, runners can encourage their teammates. Sometimes they run alone, sometimes together. After the race, the combined times of all the teammates is the team score.

In this sport, Christians can see a picture of God's plan. The fact that we are allowed to be part of the team at all is evidence of God's grace. We do not earn a place; we are joined to the team by faith in Jesus. The victory celebration to which we look forward is guaranteed by Christ. Our team has won, but we must run to finish.

Ask yourself: *Have I accepted God's gracious invitation to be part of his team by believing in Jesus Christ? Am I running to finish?*

Promised to those who love him. Christians can consider themselves truly blessed, no matter what their outward circumstances, because they have been promised the crown of life. God helps believers undergoing trials to rest and trust in him. Not only our faith, but our love for God will deepen as we endure life's trials. As we love God, his promises become ours.

1:13 We must have a correct view of God in order to persevere during times of trial. Specifically, we need to understand God's view of our temptations. Trials and temptations always present us with choices. God wants us to make good choices, not evil ones. Hardships can produce spiritual maturity and lead to eternal benefits if endured in faith. But tests can also be failed. We can give in to temptation. And when we fail, we often use all kinds of excuses and reasons for our actions. The most dangerous of these is to blame God for tempting us. James turns his attention to this problem.

When tempted. As used here, the Greek word for temptation (*peirasmos*) stands for a direct evil impulse. It can be used to indicate a trial (1:12), a temptation from within (1:14), or a temptation from without, usually relating to Satan's work (Matthew 4:1). In Jesus' best-known prayer, he told his disciples to ask God, "And do not lead us into temptation, but deliver us from the evil one" (Matthew 6:13 NKJV). It is crucial for us to remember always that God *tests* people for good; he does not *tempt* people for evil. Even during temptation we can see God's sovereignty in *permitting* Satan to tempt us in order to refine our faith and help us grow in our dependence on Christ.

No one should say, "God is tempting me." NIV Instead of persevering (1:12), we may give in or give up in the face of trial. We might even rationalize that God is at fault for sending such a trying experience, and thus blame God for our failure. From the beginning it has been a natural human response to make excuses and blame others for sin (see Genesis 3:12-13). Excuses include:

- "It's the other person's fault."

- "I couldn't help it."

- "Everybody's doing it."

- "It was just a mistake."

- "Nobody's perfect."

- "I didn't know it was wrong."

- "The devil made me do it."

- "I was pressured into it."

A person who makes excuses is trying to shift blame from himself or herself to something or someone else. A Christian, on the other hand, accepts responsibility for his or her wrongs, confesses them, and asks God for forgiveness.

For God cannot be tempted by evil. Because God cannot be tempted by evil, he cannot be the author of temptation. James is arguing against the pagan view of the gods where good and evil coexisted.

Nor does He Himself tempt anyone.ᴺᴷᴶⱽ God does not wish evil on people; he does not cause evil; he does not try to trip people up. Our failures are not God's fault. God may test believers in order to strengthen their faith, but he never tries to induce sin or destroy faith. God does not want us to fail, but to succeed. See these examples of God testing his followers: Abraham (Genesis 22:1); Israel (Judges 2:22); and King Hezekiah (2 Kings 20:12-19; 2 Chronicles 32:31).

At this point, the question may be rightly asked: "If God really loves us, why doesn't he protect us from temptation?" A God who kept us from temptation would be a God unwilling to allow us to grow. In order for a test to be an effective tool for growth, it must be capable of being failed. God actually proves his love by protecting us *in* temptation instead of protecting us *from* temptation. He provides a way to resist: "No temptation has seized you except what is common to man. And God is faithful; he will not let you be tempted beyond what you can bear. But when you are tempted, he will also provide a way out so that you can stand up under it" (1 Corinthians 10:13).

GOD'S WAY OUT OF TEMPTATION

God gives us these resources during temptation:

- *His presence.* "He will not leave you nor forsake you" (Deuteronomy 31:6 ɴᴋᴶⱽ; see also Hebrews 13:5).
- *His model—Jesus.* "For this reason he had to be made like his brothers in every way, in order that he might become a merciful and faithful high priest in service to God, and that he might make atonement for the sins of the people. Because he himself suffered when he was tempted, he is able to help those who are being tempted" (Hebrews 2:17-18 ɴɪⱽ).
- *His guidance.* "Your word is a lamp to my feet and a light for my path" (Psalm 119:105 ɴʀsⱽ).
- *His mission for our life that keeps us directed.* "Therefore, since we are surrounded by such a great cloud of witnesses, let us throw off everything that hinders and the sin that so easily entangles, and let us run with perseverance the race marked out for us" (Hebrews 12:1 ɴɪⱽ).
- *His other people with whom we share encouragement.* "And let us consider how we may spur one another on toward love and good deeds. Let us not give up meeting together, as some are in the habit of doing, but let us encourage one another—and all the more as you see the Day approaching" (Hebrews 10:24-25 ɴɪⱽ).
- *His forgiveness when we fall and fail.* "If we confess our sins, he who is faithful and just will forgive us our sins and cleanse us from all unrighteousness" (1 John 1:9 ɴʀsⱽ).

1:14 Some believers thought that since God allowed trials, he must also be the source of temptation. These people could excuse their sin by saying that God was at fault. James corrects this. Temptations come from within. Here James highlights individual responsibility for sin.

But each one is tempted when, by his own evil desire. NIV Behind the idea of the *evil desire* is the Jewish doctrine of the two *yetzers*. This has to do with the Jewish belief that all people have two *yetzers* or impulses—an impulse to good and an impulse to evil—and that these impulses war within them. It is possible, perhaps even likely, that James is building upon this Jewish idea.

The NIV adds the implied *evil* to the Greek *epithumia* (desire), which can but does not have to imply an evil craving or lust. Normal desires, such as hunger, can also be the starting point of temptation if they are allowed to control our actions. When Jesus was tempted in the wilderness (Matthew 4), the temptation came through a natural desire for food after a long fast. Satan urged Jesus to satisfy that desire in an inappropriate way, at the wrong time. The temptation was real, but Jesus did not sin by experiencing it. He would have sinned if he had given in to the devil's suggestion.

Desires can be either fed or starved. If the desire itself is evil, we must deny its wish. It is up to us, with God's help. If we encourage our desires, they will soon become actions. The blame for sin is ours alone. The kind of desire James is describing here is desire out of control. It is selfish and seductive.

Does James take Satan off the hook by placing responsibility for temptation on our desires? No, he does not. We will see later (3:15; 4:7) that the role of Satan was very much in James's thinking. Part of the answer here is in the word *by* (*hupo*), which can refer to both the agent and the cause. This same dual use is present in English. We can say "He was led by his friend" or "He was led by the hand by his friend." In the former case we are speaking of the agent doing the leading; in the latter, we are referring to the means or cause used to do the leading. Likewise, we may be led by our desires, but it is the devil behind the impulse when we are going in an evil direction.

When he is drawn away by his own desires and enticed. NKJV The enticement of evil is expressed in two ways—being dragged away or being lured like a fish to bait, and being enticed. Temptation comes from evil desires within us, not from God. We can both build and bait our own trap. It begins with an evil thought and becomes sin when we dwell on the thought and allow it to become an action. Like a snowball rolling downhill, sin grows more destructive the more we let it have its way. The best time to stop a temptation is before it is too great or moving too fast to control. (See Matthew 4:1-11; 1 Corinthians 10:13; and 2 Timothy 2:22 for more about escaping temptation.)

So we meet the enemy called temptation and discover it is in us. How can we withstand the attacks we know will come?

- We must continually place ourselves under God's protection (see the spiritual resources listed under the notes for 1:13).

- We must reject the enticement, or temptation by recognizing it as a false promise.

- We must bring into our life those activities that we know God has provided for our benefit—knowledge of Scripture, fellowship with Christ and other believers, good music, appreciation of all God has made—activities that expand our awareness in life.

THE DEVIL AND OUR DESIRES

How does the devil make our desires serve his purposes?

- He offers suggestions from within our environment and experience. What seems at first glance to be harmless may lead to evil. The person who takes Satan's suggestions into his mind is fighting on dangerous ground. But the devil can't entice our mind against our will.

- He deceives with false advertising. Fame, sex, wealth, and power are presented to us as though they satisfy. But we don't have to take his suggestions.

- He singles us out through fear, making us feel as though we are struggling alone. But we are warned to "Be self-controlled and alert. Your enemy the devil prowls around like a roaring lion looking for someone to devour" (1 Peter 5:8 NIV). Knowing that we have these potential weaknesses in our defenses should motivate us to be careful to control our desires.

1:15 **Then, when that desire has conceived, it gives birth to sin.**NRSV James traces the result of temptation when a person yields to it. Desire in itself is not sin, but assenting to its enticement eventually gives birth to sin. Note that the first two steps in the process (desiring and conceiving) emphasize the internal nature of sin. The sequence, described clearly in sexual language, represents the course any sins have taken by the time they are apparent to others. Since it begins within, the help we need the most in combating sin is internal. That help comes from God. The best time to stop sin is at the moment we realize the desire is about to become focused, before it has conceived.

It takes spiritual growth and consistent dependence on God to know when a desire can be calmly evaluated and when a desire can easily become lustful and controlling. Desires that present themselves to us in expressions that begin with "I have to have," "I can't do without," or even "I would do anything if only I could" are all ripe for conception and birth into sin. It is helpful to ask ourselves occasionally, "What reasoning do I use that tends to lead me into sin?"

And sin, when it is full-grown, gives birth to death.[NIV] Life is given to those who persevere in trials (1:12); death comes to those who allow their desire to run its course. Sin is *full-grown* when it becomes a fixed habit. *Death* is referring to spiritual separation from God that comes as the result of sin (see also Romans 6:23; 7:7-12; 1 John 2:16-17; 3:14).

When we yield to temptation, our sin sets deadly events into motion. There is more to stopping *sin* than just stopping *sinning.* Damage has been done. Deciding to "sin no more" may take care of the future, but it does not heal the past. That healing must come through repentance and forgiveness. Sometimes restitution must be made. As serious as the remedy sounds, we can be deeply grateful that there is a remedy at all. God loves us. It is his

At first it [temptation] is a mere thought confronting the mind; then imagination paints it in stronger colors; only after that do we take pleasure in it, and the will makes a false move, and we give our assent.

Thomas à Kempis

THE TWO WAYS

There is a way that seems right to a person, but its end is the way to death (Proverbs 14:12 NRSV).

Desire
↕
Temptation
↕
Lust/Sin
↕
Habitual Sin
↕
Death

Jesus answered, "I am the way, and the truth, and the life. No one comes to the Father except through me" (John 14:6 NRSV).

Trial
↕
Faith
↕
Obedience
↕
Perseverance
↕
Crown of life

gracious love that breaks the cycle of desire-sin-death. Wherever we find ourselves in the process, we can turn to God in repentance for help. His way leads to life.

1:16 Do not be deceived. The Greek expression means "stop being deceived"—deceived about God's goodness and about the source of temptation. Simply claiming that God is not the author of evil doesn't automatically mean that he will help us fight it. If life was fully defined by 1:13-15, our situation would be desperate. We might be faced with struggling against sin while God watched, uninvolved either way. James hurries on to spell out our hope. Not only does God *not* tempt us, he is also actively providing everything good that we find in life. We are not to attribute evil intent to God—God is the source of good gifts, especially the new birth (1:18). He is the author of salvation, not temptation. Paragraph 1:16-18 is the positive side of the picture painted in 1:13-15.

The danger behind James's warning to us not to be deceived is the temptation to believe that God does not care, or won't help us, or may even be working against us. The picture is not pretty. If we come to believe we are alone, we have been deceived. If we distrust God, we have been deceived. And if we dare to accuse God of being the tempter, we have been thoroughly deceived.

What more devastating example of deception could there be than seeing the source of all good as the source of evil? Is it any wonder that Jesus leveled this charge at those who had a twisted view of God? "You belong to your father, the devil, and you want to carry out your father's desire. He was a murderer from the beginning, not holding to the truth, for there is no truth in him. When he lies, he speaks his native language, for he is a liar and the father of lies" (John 8:44). Believing in God is important, but it also matters how we believe in him. As James will illustrate later (2:19), we are capable of believing in God—the wrong way. It is this very deception that James is attacking by his entire letter.

My dear brothers.NIV The phrase is literally "my beloved brothers." It both softens and directs the warning. James mixes even the hard statements that he must write with reminders of the love behind his letter. People will listen to hard things more readily when they are reminded that the one saying them is doing so out of genuine love.

1:17 So how can we keep from falling into temptation? The way is found in a close relationship with God and the application of his

Word to daily life. This pattern will lead us to see clearly that every good and perfect gift is from above.

Every good gift and perfect gift is from above. NKJV In contrast to the view that God sends evil, James points out here that: (1) God is the source of everything good, and (2) God's good gifts are also perfect. This part of the verse can also be translated, "Every generous act of giving, with every perfect gift" (NRSV). As is so often the case with the Bible, the meaning of the words is good news even at first reading, and the meaning gets better as we understand it. God is not only the source of good gifts, he is the very source of the giving impulse.

The ability to give is one aspect of God's image in us. And God's gifts are also perfect. They are good gifts, given at the right time, for good purposes. This can result in God withholding a good gift from us that would not be perfect for us. That same gift may be perfect for someone else. This truth should help us rejoice with others when they receive good gifts from God even though we have not received the same ones.

We can be assured that God always wills the best for us—not good things today and bad things tomorrow. Whatever happens is for our best. God is not like the well-meaning relative who gives the beautiful, warm coat we have always wanted, but that is unfortunately several sizes too small. God's gifts are very good, and they also fit us perfectly.

Coming down from the Father of lights. NRSV This phrase pictures God as the sovereign Creator of the sun, moon, and stars (see Genesis 1; Isaiah 60:19-22; and John 1:1-14.) The giving character of God is written into his creation. "The heavens declare the glory of God; the skies proclaim the work of his hands" (Psalm 19:1). God gives us good gifts—and the light by which to see and enjoy them.

Who does not change like shifting shadows. NIV God's character is always trustworthy and reliable (Malachi 3:6). Nothing can block God's goodness from reaching us. What does not change about God is his giving nature. It is constant and consistent. He is undaunted by our inconsistencies and unfaithfulness. We may be like shifting shadows, but God remains the Father of lights. It is

---

Light of the world! for
ever, ever shining
There is no change
in Thee;
True Light of Life, all joy
and health enshrining,
Thou canst not fade
nor flee.
Horatius Bonar

---

a healthy exercise in humility to express our gratefulness to God for his unchanging love towards us.

1:18 **He gave us birth by the word of truth.** NRSV This is a shining example of the good things God gives ("every good and perfect gift")—he gives us spiritual birth! We are saved because God chose to save us. Our spiritual birth is not by accident or because he *had* to. The *birth* is the new birth given to all believers (see John 3:3-8; Romans 12:2; Ephesians 1:5; Titus 3:5; 1 Peter 1:3, 23; 1 John 3:9). The *word of truth* is the gospel, the Good News of salvation (Ephesians 1:13; Colossians 1:5; 2 Timothy 2:15). We hear about the gift of birth through the reading and preaching of the gospel, and we respond to it. We apply the message to ourselves and our needs. We receive the offered gift. It is God's gift as he gives it and becomes our gift when we receive it.

That we might be a kind of firstfruits of His creatures. NKJV Jewish leaders would be well aware of the practice of offering the first crops to ripen just prior to harvest as an act of worship and as a blessing on the rest of the harvest (see Exodus 34:22; Leviticus 23:9-10; Deuteronomy 26:9-11). Believers are firstfruits because we are a new creation in Christ; we are no longer sinners separated from God, but God's own children (Romans 8:19-23; 1 Corinthians 15:20-23; 2 Thessalonians 2:13). The rest of all he created must wait for God's plan to unfold, but those who have been given spiritual birth have been welcomed by the first firstfruit, Christ (1 Corinthians 15:20), into the kingdom of God and are part of the new creation that he has established. As Paul expresses it, "We know that the whole creation has been groaning as in the pains of childbirth right up to the present time. Not only so, but we ourselves, who have the firstfruits of the Spirit, groan inwardly as we wait eagerly for our adoption as sons, the redemption of our bodies" (Romans 8:22-23 NIV). Though we have been given spiritual birth we live in a world that has not yet been transformed. Living as firstfruits (examples of God's goodness and role models of what he can do in a life) in a fallen world ought to be our overriding desire. The letter of James could be subtitled, "How to live as a firstfruit!"

LISTENING AND DOING / 1:19-27

James has spoken of the new birth; he now explains that this new birth should reveal itself in the way we act. He has also connected the new birth with its source, God's Word. The ongoing importance of that Word will be the subject of the next paragraph. The Word that brings us life also guides us in living the life it has brought to us. From the grand scope of God's eternal plan and the unique place of believers in creation, James turns to the painful and practical essentials of living as "firstfruits."

1:19 My dear brothers, take note of this. NIV James begins with a single, attention-getting Greek word: *Iste* (know!), translated "take note of this." It has the same effect as when we say, "Listen!" before saying something we don't want people to miss. Verse 19 records the theme for the rest of the chapter. Again James reminds his reader that these are family rules of conduct ("dear brothers").

Let everyone be quick to listen. NRSV When James speaks to *everyone* here, he is especially referring to teachers (see 3:1). What they need to listen to is God's Word (1:18). The expression *quick to listen* is a beautiful way of capturing the idea of active listening. We are not simply to refrain from speaking; we are to be ready and willing to listen. *Quick* also implies a readiness to obey what we hear. We often find the attitude among believers that the speaker is entirely responsible for getting the people to listen by being entertaining, relevant, and engaging. James shifts the responsibility back to the audience. This "quick" listening is obviously to be done with discernment. We are to check what we hear with God's Word. If we don't listen both carefully and quickly, we are liable to be led into all kinds of false teaching and error.

> We have two ears but only one mouth, that we may hear more and speak less.
>
> *Zeno*

Slow to speak. Quick to listen and slow to speak should be taken together as sides of the same coin. Slowness in speaking means speaking with humility and patience, not with hasty words or nonstop gabbing. Constant talking keeps a person from being able to hear. Wisdom is not always having something to say; it involves listening carefully, considering prayerfully, and speaking quietly. When we talk too much and listen too little, we communicate to others that we think our ideas are much more important than theirs. James wisely advises us to reverse this process. We need to put a mental stopwatch on our conversations and keep track of how much we talk and how much we listen. When people talk to us, do they feel that their viewpoints and ideas have value?

Teachers are especially prone to an imbalance when it comes to speaking and listening. We should take careful note of the way

Jesus mixed the two. His speaking tended to be marked by brevity. He asked questions. He listened. We should ask ourselves, "Have I listened enough to know that what I've said was heard?"

Slow to anger.^{NRSV} Anger closes our minds to God's truth (see an example in 2 Kings 5:11; see also Proverbs 10:19; 13:3; 17:28; 29:20). It is anger that erupts when our egos are bruised—"I am hurt"; "My opinions are not being heard." It is just the kind of anger that rises from too much fast talking and not enough quick listening!

When injustice and sin occur, we *should* become angry because others are being hurt. But we should not become angry when we fail to win an argument, or when we feel offended or neglected. Selfish anger never helps anybody (see Ecclesiastes 7:9; Matthew 5:21-26; Ephesians 4:26).

1:20 **Man's anger does not bring about the righteous life that God desires.**^{NIV} The anger spoken of here is a thoughtless, uncontrolled temper that leads to rash, hurtful words. Our anger toward others does not create within us a life that can withstand God's scrutiny. Why not? Because expressed anger tends to be uncontrollable. Anger is inconsistent with Jesus' command to love our enemies (Matthew 5:43-48) and not hate our brothers (Matthew 5:21-26). Anger usurps God's role as judge. In fact, we can be sure our anger is wrong when it keeps us from living as God wants us to live.

So how can we obtain the righteous life that God desires? If we were to ask this question to James at this point in his letter, he would probably send us back to the beginning. The righteous life that God desires avoids anger, but actively pursues the following: tested faith, endurance, maturity, perfection, contentment, spiritual birth, quick listening, and obeying God's Word.

WHERE ANGER ERUPTS

Knowing the places and the ways that we are tempted can help us prepare by praying and by planning alternative responses instead of giving in to anger:

- *Family*—When we are misunderstood, ignored, unloved, criticized
- *Church*—When we are unnoticed, overlooked, unappreciated, criticized
- *Workplace*—When we are slighted, overworked, harassed, criticized
- *Friends*—When we are left out, disappointed, criticized
- *Society*—When we feel singled out for unfairness, taxed, criticized

1:21 **Get rid of all moral filth and the evil that is so prevalent.** NIV According to the Greek, this is a once-for-all action. Why should we do this? Progress in our spiritual life cannot occur unless we see sin for what it is, quit justifying it, and decide to reject it. James's word picture here has us getting rid of our evil habits and actions like stripping off dirty clothes.

Receive with meekness the implanted word. NKJV Humble acceptance is contrasted with the quick speech and anger from 1:19. James is not asking believers to be converted—that has already happened. To accept the planted word he speaks of here is to accept its laws as binding and to seek to live by them. We are not to look for something to argue about, but with humility to live by that word. Yet we are not to be so "humble" that we feel unworthy to live by God's Word and thus decide not to try—that is false humility and does not honor God. To humbly accept the word, we must be "quick to listen" (good listeners), "slow to speak" (thoughtful), "slow to anger" (not hasty and jumping to conclusions), and willing to do what it says (1:19).

The word is *planted* in us when it becomes part of our being. God teaches us from the depths of our soul, from the teaching of the Spirit, and by the teaching of Spirit-led people. The soil in which the word is planted must be hospitable in order for it to grow. To make our soil hospitable, we must give up any impurities in our life. The exchange James describes, where we remove the sin covering our life and accept what has been planted within, helps us understand several ways that God works. God's Word directs us in identifying and removing those things that are unacceptable in our life. His Word and Spirit also work inside us. Our spiritual growth happens from the inside out. A wound must have its surface cleaned and kept clean until a scab forms, but healing occurs from the inside out. This verse describes both aspects of this process applied to our spiritual life.

Which is able to save your souls. NKJV Christians are not finished with God's Word once we are saved. Instead, God's Word becomes a permanent part of us, guiding us through each day. The implanted Word becomes part of us; then we absorb the characteristics taught in the Word; then these are expressed in living. Trials and temptations cannot defeat us if we are applying God's truth to our life.

1:22 **Do not merely listen to the word.** NIV The *word* is the gospel taught by Jesus and proclaimed by his followers. Simply reading, even studying, God's Word does not profit us if we don't do what it says. We learn God's Word not just to *know* it, but also to *do* it.

And so deceive yourselves.^{NIV} It is self-deception to congratulate ourselves about knowledge of Scripture if that's all there is to it. This is the second kind of deception that James warns against. In 1:16 he tells us not to be deceived about God's character. Here James is concerned that we not be deceived about the character of God's Word. We are not to engage in passive listening, but rather in an active attentiveness that leads to action.

> Obedience is the mother of true knowledge of God.
>
> *John Calvin*

Be doers of the word.^{NKJV} Worthwhile knowledge is a prelude to action; God's Word can only grow in the soil of obedience. In order for a lesson to make a difference in a student's life, it must enter the heart and mind, affecting his or her life. It is important to hear God's Word, but it is much more important to obey it. We can measure the effectiveness of our Bible study time by the effect it has on our behavior and attitudes. Do we put into action what we have studied?

> Passive Christianity is morally wrong.
>
> *Bruce Barton*

The emphasis on listening combined with doing is found elsewhere in the New Testament. Paul wrote: "For it is not the hearers of the law who are righteous in God's sight, but the doers of the law who will be justified" (Romans 2:13 NRSV). Jesus himself said, "Blessed rather are those who hear the word of God and obey it" (Luke 11:28 NRSV). James may well have heard his half brother, Jesus, talk about obedience many times. Here James, too, is emphasizing the importance of actions as part of faith. Later, he will discuss this topic at length (2:14-26).

Meanwhile, we can begin to examine how we might fall under James's concern. How often do we merely "hear" the Word with no intention whatsoever of obeying it? If our actions of service are only self-serving and our concern only for those closest to us, we are not being obedient to Jesus. In his scathing story of the final judgment (Matthew 25:31-46), Jesus points out that "Whatever you did for one of the least of these brothers of mine, you did for me" (Matthew 25:40 NIV).

1:23-24 **Anyone who listens to the word but does not do what it says is like a man who looks at his face in a mirror and, after looking at himself, goes away and immediately forgets what he looks like.**^{NIV} These and the following verses show different ways of handling God's Word. Some people take a casual look at God's Word without letting it affect their lives, like the person who looks so quickly into a mirror that flaws go undetected and nothing is changed. They listen but don't act. The other approach is the intent look, the deep and continued study of God's Word that allows a person to see flaws and change his or her life in line with God's standards.

The repeated use of the word *listens* is significant. It reminds us of the difference in literacy between today and the first century. Most of the audience to whom James was writing probably did not read the Scriptures themselves but were accustomed to hearing the Scriptures read aloud. Their exposure to God's Word was through repeatedly hearing it read until they had memorized it. Note, for instance, Paul's counsel to Timothy: "Until I come, devote yourself to the public reading of Scripture, to preaching and to teaching" (1 Timothy 4:13 NIV).

The verbs *looking* and *forgets* picture something that naturally or repeatedly occurs. *Goes away* pictures casualness and immediacy—at once he is gone and forgets. It would be silly to leave dirt on your face or your hair in a mess after seeing yourself in a mirror. It is just as silly to look into God's Word and make no changes in your life. Whether we read God's Word for ourselves or hear it read, our listening must have an attitude of seriousness and submission that will lead to obedience.

BARRIERS TO LISTENING
Certain approaches or attitudes almost ensure that we will not be listening carefully to God's Word:
- Some are able to read God's Word, but don't, or won't.
- Some rely on an outdated translation of Scripture that is difficult to understand.
- Some allow so many distractions that they cannot possibly listen.
- Some are not accountable to anyone for their obedience to God's Word.
- Some have become insensitive to their need for spiritual input.

1:25 The man who looks intently . . . and continues to do this. NIV This man looks with serious attention and then makes God's law his chosen lifestyle. He studies with rapt attention not only once, but continuously; as a result, he remembers God's Word and does what it says. The mirror of God's Word has shown his flaws, so he can correct them.

The kind of mirror that God's Word provides is unique. It shows us our inner nature in the same way that a regular mirror shows our exterior features. Both mirrors reflect what is there. When God's Word points out something in us that needs correction, we had better listen and act.

Into the perfect law of liberty. NKJV This law is perfect because:

- It is God's law.
- It cannot be improved.
- It works toward a given end.

SEVEN WAYS TO LISTEN INTENTLY TO GOD'S WORD
An intent look at God's Word is more likely to help us than casual attention will:

1. Read the Bible aloud to yourself with expression.
2. Use small cards with verses printed on them to refer to throughout the day.
3. Whenever a verse includes a command, think of at least three ways you can put that command into action that same day.
4. Ask someone else (maybe even a Christian that you don't know very well) to comment on the verse that you are trying to understand and obey.
5. Ask for an explanation when someone mentions a verse or passage you do not understand.
6. Memorize sections of God's Word.
7. Meditate on the parts of God's Word you have memorized.

The law gives freedom because it is only in obeying God's law that true freedom can be found (compare John 8:31-32). Obeying our emotions and giving in to all our desires is true slavery. But in accepting God's will, we are truly free to be what God created us to be. Believers respond to God because they want to, not because they have to. We are free to obey (1 Corinthians 9:20; Galatians 5:13; 6:2).

> To obey God is liberty.
>
> *Seneca*

What exactly is this *perfect law?* Elsewhere in James he calls it the "royal law" (2:8). It is the foundational principle that the Lord Jesus spelled out: "'Love the Lord your God with all your heart and with all your soul and with all your mind.' This is the first and greatest commandment. And the second is like it: 'Love your neighbor as yourself.' All the Law and the Prophets hang on these two commandments" (Matthew 22:37-40 NIV). The perfect law calls us to love God unconditionally and to love others as we would ourselves. It is a law with almost unlimited applications. Jesus expanded on some of those applications in the Sermon on the Mount (Matthew 5–7), many echoes of which are found in James. In John 8:31-32, Jesus pointed out how knowing and obeying his teachings brings freedom.

It seems paradoxical that a law could give us freedom, but

God's law points out sin in us and gives us the opportunity to ask for God's forgiveness (see Romans 7:7-8). As Christians, we are saved by God's grace, and salvation frees us from sin's control. As believers we are free to live as God created us to live. Of course, this does not mean that we are free to do as we please (1 Peter 2:16)—we are now free to obey God.

THE PIANO PLAYER

A little child sits enraptured, watching his mother play the piano. The music is thrilling. As her fingers fly over the keys, he recognizes simple melodies and then listens with amazement as she embellishes them with harmony and chords until there is only a hint of their original simplicity.

The child finally crawls up on the bench next to his mother and waits for her to stop. He wants a turn. Expecting to produce what he heard Mother play, he moves his fingers over the keys in imitation. The chaos of sound is pure freedom, unbound by such things as a coherent tune, order, or music theory. For a moment it is fun to make noise, but noise gets dreary. "When can I play like you, Mommy?" he asks.

"After a while," she answers, remembering all those boring lessons and the endless drills and scales. Then she smiles as she remembers those glorious days when, having somehow internalized all those lessons, she suddenly realized she was actually, wonderfully, *freely* playing the piano. The freedom to play only came through learning and practicing the law of the piano.

This one will be blessed in what he does.NKJV The person is blessed because:

- He looks intently at God's Word.

- He continues to do this.

- He does not forget what he has heard.

- He acts on it, letting it make a difference in his life.

- He then reaps the benefits of having done what God required.

1:26 God's perfect law should be put into practice in our speech. Here James introduces two major themes that he will discuss at length later: the use of the tongue (3:1-12) and the treatment of the unfortunate (throughout the letter).

If anyone considers himself religious and yet does not keep a tight rein on his tongue.NIV Knowing how to speak well—as a great teacher would—is not nearly as important as having control of our speech: knowing what to say and where and when to say it. If our faith only makes us consider ourselves religious, then it's not worth much. If we valued our faith, there would be evidence in our actions. James is repeating the direction given in 1:19, to be "slow to speak," but this time with an equestrian twist. The way that others will know whether or not our faith is real is by what we choose to talk about and the way we speak.

How, then, do we keep a tight rein on our tongue? Based on what James has told us so far, we can be sure that we will not be able to talk our way out of this problem. The beginning of developing a tight rein is putting into action the negative and positive actions that are required in 1:21: "Therefore, get rid of all moral filth and the evil that is so prevalent and humbly accept the word planted in you, which can save you." One of the ways that the "moral filth and evil" become apparent to others is by what flows from our mouth. Jesus explained this fact in refuting the emphasis on mere ritual cleanliness that was so important in his day. Jesus said, "What comes out of a man is what makes him 'unclean.' For from within, out of men's hearts, come evil thoughts, sexual immorality, theft, murder, adultery, greed, malice, deceit, lewdness, envy, slander, arrogance and folly. All these evils come from inside and make a man 'unclean'" (Mark 7:20-23 NIV). We must keep from expressing this evil when we speak. (For more on the control of the tongue, see 3:1-12.)

He deceives himself and his religion is worthless.[NIV] It is self-deception to have religious practices that do not lead to an ethical lifestyle. In this verse, James points out a third dangerous deception: (1) we are deceived when we believe a distorted view of the character of God (1:16); (2) we are deceived when we listen to God's Word without taking action (1:22); and (3) we are deceived when we accept our own rationalization that our beliefs can be kept inside or expressed in ritual with no real obedience.

Even our outward religious practices are worthless without obedience. And we cannot be obedient if we cannot control our mouth. James does not specify how the tongue offends, but we can imagine a series of ways that our tongue dishonors God— gossip, angry outbursts, harsh criticism, complaining, judging. When we let our tongue wag that way, our spiritual pronouncements and practices become worthless. Our verbal actions speak louder than our religious rituals. When both prove to be false, they merit the title of *worthless* that James gives them. Pretending to be religious and convincing ourselves that we are is not only deceptive to others, it is also a deadly self-deception. Conversion

JAMES 1:27

38

is meaningless unless it leads to a changed life. A changed life goes nowhere unless it serves others.

James presents a powerful challenge to a world more and more tolerant of the idea that religion is whatever the individual makes it—self-designed faith is worthless. Believing in a God we refuse to submit to or obey is just another expression of sinful rebellion. In the end, it does not matter whether we consider ourselves religious. The real question is, What does God consider us to be?

1:27 From a religion easily capable of rationalizing any behavior, James now turns to a relationship where God is allowed to direct the terms of behavior—**Religion . . . pure and undefiled.** NRSV James explains religion in terms of practical service and personal purity. Rituals done with reverence are not wrong; but if a person still refuses to obey God in daily life, his "religion" is not accepted by God. What *is* accepted by God? Acceptable religion is practical. Outward rituals cannot substitute for outward righteousness. Church services are no substitute for our *service* to God. Inward rationalizations are no substitute for inward righteousness. Telling ourselves that God is not aware of our real attitude towards him and his Word is, as James keeps reminding us, self-deception.

Pure and faultless religion is not perfect observance of rules and observances; instead, it is a spirit that pervades our hearts and lives (Leviticus 19:18; Isaiah 1:16-17). Like Jesus, James explains religion in terms of a vital inner faith that acts itself out in daily life. Our conduct must be in keeping with our faith (1 Corinthians 5:8). This verse is not intended to be an exhaustive definition of Christianity. Instead, it characterizes conduct that is important to Christianity. It contrasts with mere acts of worship that are commonly called "religion." In fact, the point becomes clear that the more obviously "religious" a behavior is, the more easily it becomes meaningless, while some of the most humble and common actions are the greatest opportunities for worshipful obedience. These are acts that we probably would not do except out of obedience to God. Jesus' touching lepers when he healed them is a vivid example of this type of action. James presents two simple and practical actions of obedient faith that almost anyone can take.

To care for orphans and widows in their distress. NRSV This is an illustration of how our Christian *conduct* should look. Orphans and widows are often mentioned in the concerns of the early church because these were the most obviously "poor" in first-century Israel. The widows, because they had no access to inheritances in Jewish circles, were very much on the outskirts of society. This is why Paul had to develop an entire order concerning widows in his own churches, as in 1 Timothy 5. The widows could not get jobs, and their inheritances went to their oldest sons. It was expected that the widows would be taken care of by their own families, and so the Jews left them with very little economic support. Unless a family member was willing to care for them, they were reduced to begging, selling themselves as slaves, or starving. By caring for these powerless people, the church put God's Word into practice. When we give with no hope of receiving in return, we show what it means to serve others.

Even today, the presence of widows and orphans in our communities and cities makes this directive of James very contemporary. To this group we can also add those who have become de facto widows and orphans through the death of families in divorce. These people have complicated lives. The needs always threaten to overwhelm our human resources. Looking after hurting people is stressful work. Yet we are called to be involved. James balances the command to be concerned about others with the command to be concerned about our own life.

To keep oneself unstained by the world. NRSV This is a picture of how our Christian *character* should look. To keep ourselves from being polluted by the world, we need to commit ourselves to Christ's ethical and moral system, not the world's. We are not to adapt to the world's value system based on money, power, and pleasure. True faith means nothing if we are contaminated with such values. James was simply echoing the words of Jesus in what has been called his "high priestly" prayer (John 17), where Jesus emphasized sending his disciples *into* the world but expecting them not to be *of* the world. The heart of Jesus' prayer was, "My prayer is not that you take them out of the world but that you protect them from the evil one" (John 17:15 NIV). As we make ourselves available to serve Christ in the world, we must keep putting ourselves under the protection of this prayer. It helps to replace the two "them" words with our name as we visualize Jesus praying for us. The prayer makes two important points: (1) we remain in the world because that is where Christ wants us; and (2) we will have God's protection.

James 2

DO NOT FAVOR THE RICH / 2:1-13

James 1:19-27 encourages us to put our beliefs into practice. In 2:1-13, James gives a practical lesson: we are not to show favoritism. Such discrimination violates God's truth.

James is persuasive. James wants his readers to wake up and live right. He wants our faith to work its way into all our relationships.

As the Christian faith outgrew its Jewish roots, it was in danger of perpetuating certain customs that might have seemed beneficial but were in fact deadly. In the existing synagogues, it was the tradition to give places of honor to those who had earned them in some way. What may have originally started out of respect for the wisdom of leaders eventually became a system of status and power within local synagogues. James and others realized what a profoundly destructive effect this kind of elitism would have on the gospel. Christ came to set people free. The law to which James refers is not the ceremonial, superficial law of religious people, but the "law that gives freedom" (1:25). Favoritism brings bondage.

James actually almost takes welcoming strangers for granted. He is urging us to be alert about the *way* that we welcome strangers into the church. He does not want the warmth or honor of our welcome to be determined by the status or apparent wealth of the visitor. It is showing favoritism based on social standing that James specifically condemns. He makes it a cause for questioning the reality of a person's faith.

2:1 My brothers.^{NIV} The readers were members of the church and his dear brothers in the Christian faith. James addresses his brothers because what he is explaining is a family issue. Among believers in Christ there exists a common accountability to God's Word. Whenever we remind one another of something Jesus taught, it must be done in such a way that we remember we are also required to obey. Biblical truth applies to all of us. By saying "my brothers," James emphasizes the togetherness of real obedience to Christ.

As believers in our glorious Lord Jesus Christ. NIV James appeals to a single fact that binds these people together—they are all believers. His reference is not to common human values or general goodwill, but rather to the strongest bond that believers claim. The family relationship he is describing is limited to those who believe in our glorious Lord Jesus Christ.

Early Christians developed descriptions for Jesus that expressed the depth of their trust in him. They could be called reflective names, since they resulted from reflections on Jesus. Paul gives us a number of his reflective names for Jesus:

- his Son, Jesus Christ our Lord (1 Corinthians 1:9)

- Christ, the power of God and the wisdom of God (1 Corinthians 1:24)

- the image of the invisible God (Colossians 1:15)

- the beginning and the firstborn from among the dead (Colossians 1:18)

- our great God and Savior, Jesus Christ (Titus 2:13)

Some of these became significant as titles for Christ. This exercise of designing personal descriptions of Christ can be a beneficial discipline for a Christian. It helps us focus on what Christ means to us. For example, each of the terms in James's title conveys an aspect of his understanding of Christ's unique role:

- The one in whom we believe is *ours.* There is personal ownership and relationship. A significant line has been crossed when a person can say, not only "Jesus is Lord," but also "Jesus is *my* Lord." And a believer ought always to seek fellowship with others so they can say together, "Jesus is *our* Lord."

- The one in whom we believe is *glorious.* The word relates to the impression Christ made on people when they realized who he was. John made Christ's glory the most convincing aspect of his incarnation: "The Word became flesh and made his dwelling among us. We have seen his glory, the glory of the One and Only, who came from the Father, full of grace and truth" (John 1:14 NIV). *Glorious* describes the divine nature of Christ, expressed even in his humanity.

- The one in whom we believe is *Lord.* The effectiveness of seeing ourselves as servants depends on who we see as master. This Greek word (*kurios*) for "master" or "owner" came to be used frequently to refer to God. Jesus specifically claimed the title (Matthew 7:21-22; Mark 5:19; Luke 19:30-31; John

13:13-14). In the New Testament church, "Lord" rapidly came to refer to Jesus in his role as Master of persons and creation. It is a term believers use to express their submission to Christ.

- The one in whom we believe is *Jesus*. Mary (Luke 1:26-33) and Joseph (Matthew 1:18-21) were each told to give the unique child born of a virgin the name *Jesus*. In each case, the reason given related to a different aspect of his purpose in coming to earth. Mary was told, Jesus "will be great and will be called the Son of the Most High" (Luke 1:32 NRSV) while Joseph was told, "he will save his people from their sins" (Matthew 1:21 NRSV). The name *Jesus* means "Yahweh saves" or "Yahweh the Savior." No other name stands so clearly for Christ's dual nature as the God-man. Jesus often called himself Son of Man while at the same time claiming God was his father. When we read that Christ promises we can "ask . . . anything in my name" (John 14:14), we shouldn't be surprised at the reverence with which this name is said by believers.

- The one in whom we believe is *Christ*. *Christos* was the Greek word used to translate the word *messiah* (anointed one) from Hebrew. In the early church *Christ* rapidly became as much a name as a title for Jesus—he was the promised Savior. At the time John wrote his Gospel (c. A.D. 85), he felt it necessary to translate *Messias* (a transliteration from Hebrew into Greek) as *Christos* (see John 1:41; 4:25), for this term was more familiar to the Gentiles.

Because of their shared position as believers, James's readers were to follow the instructions he was about to give them. At times all of us need to be held accountable to our claims. If we want to be called Christians, believers in Christ, then our life needs to display the effects of that belief. There may be times when we must act with no other reason than obedience to Christ. We cannot be so identified with our society that we are unable to stand against it for the sake of Christ. Believers have established a history of resisting such evils as the imprisonment of Jews during World War II, discrimination and racism in the sixties, and abortions in the eighties, sometimes in radical opposition to societal norms.

Don't show favoritism.[NIV] Another translation would be "Stop showing favoritism." The construction of the Greek shows that James was forbidding a practice already in progress. This phrase has also been translated, "My brothers and sisters, do you with your acts of favoritism really believe in our glorious Lord Jesus

Christ?" (NRSV). The believers receiving this letter were already guilty of practicing discrimination. The believers apparently were judging people based only on externals—physical appearance, status, wealth, power; as a result, they were pandering to and being unduly influenced by people who represented these positions of prestige.

In general, social distinctions did not exist in the early church. Masters sat beside their slaves during worship; sometimes a slave was the leader of the assembly. But from its beginnings, the church had many poor, outcasts, and those of little class or influence. So when a rich person was converted, the church members needed to guard against making more of a fuss over him or her than they would at the conversion of another poor person.

Upon what grounds did James make this command? Because impartiality is an *attribute of God* (Deuteronomy 10:17; Acts 10:34; Romans 2:11; Galatians 2:6; Ephesians 6:9; Colossians 3:25); impartiality was *an attitude Jesus practiced* (Matthew 22:16; Mark 12:14; Luke 20:21); Scripture had *warned against favoritism* (Leviticus 19:15; Deuteronomy 1:17; Psalm 82:2; Proverbs 18:5). James emphasized two clear points:

1. Shunning the poor contrasts with God's attitude because he chose the poor to be rich in faith (2:5).

2. Favoritism goes against God's royal law to "Love your neighbor as yourself" (2:8). Showing favoritism based on external considerations is inconsistent with faith in Christ, who breaks down the barriers of race, class, gender, and religion (Colossians 3:11).

James's command remains important for churches today. Often we treat a well-dressed, impressive-looking person better than someone who looks poor. We do this because we would rather identify with successful people than with apparent failures. The irony, as James reminds us, is that the supposed winners may have gained their impressive lifestyle at our expense. Our churches should show no partiality with regard to people's outward appearance, wealth, or power. The law of love must rule all our attitudes toward others. Too often preferential treatment is given to the rich or powerful when offices for the church need to be filled. Too often, a church brushes aside the suggestions of its more humble or poorer members in favor of the ideas of the wealthy. Such discrimination has no place in our churches.

2:2   If a person . . . comes into your assembly. NRSV James launches into a vivid hypothetical case study. Two men were entering a meeting. We can assume that these men were both visiting, since they are described only by appearance. The meeting was either a gathering of Jewish Christians or a meeting of the Jewish synagogue. The Greek word *sunagoge* (meeting or assembly) generally refers to an assembly of people meeting for various purposes. In some instances the meeting was for legal purposes—in most instances, for worship. At the time James was writing, many Jewish Christians still worshiped on Saturday, the Jewish Sabbath, and they still called their assembly a "synagogue."

DOES YOUR CHURCH SHOW FAVORITISM?
Ask these questions:

- How closely does our congregation reflect the socioeconomic and racial neighborhood in which we gather?
- In our church, people may not be ushered to good or bad seats, but in what other ways might we be favoring the rich or discriminating against the poor?
- Would a poor person feel welcome in our church? Would a rich person feel welcome in our church?
- In what ways do we consciously or unconsciously favor some people over others in our church? Why do we do this?
- How can our ministry reach out to all people without any hint of discrimination?
- What can we do to be completely free from being impressed by the wealth or power of others?

With gold rings, in fine apparel. NKJV One man was rich, as noted by his clothing and jewelry. A ring signified upper class and power. Rings were the same kind of visible status symbols that cars function as today. The rich man here is not a Christian (as in 1:9-11) but is a non-Christian Jew (as in 2:6-7).

And a poor man in filthy clothes. NKJV This poor man was dressed in filthy rags; he was most likely a beggar. James makes it very clear that the action about to be taken, if not guarded against, will be based entirely on the appearance of these two guests. The motive or attitude of the visitors does not come into question in this case study. Neither we nor the church members can know at first glance why these two people decided to come to the meeting.

Depending on the size of a church, the arrival of a visitor can have an electric effect. Sometimes panic sets in. The rush to welcome can be overwhelming to the newcomer. But whether the greeting is reserved or enthusiastic, what is most clearly communicated is its genuineness. Individual Christians can have a significant ministry in looking for newcomers of any kind in church and making them feel welcome. The decision to follow Christ has often been made easier by a warm and honest welcome at the door of a church.

2:3 You pay attention to the one wearing the fine clothes. NKJV The rich man was shown special attention—the Greek word meaning "to look with favor on" a person. The believers were impressed by him. He became the object of special service and deference.

And say to him, "You sit here in a good place."NKJV The rich man was singled out and escorted to a comfortable and favored seat.

Say to the poor man, "You stand there" or "Sit here at my footstool."NKJV The poor man gets standing room only, or a seat on the floor. It's as if he is being told to stay apart from his "betters" by allowing them the seats, while he is given neither dignity or comfort.

The Jews had a practice of seating the most important people nearest the sacred scrolls. Other people would be seated in the back. This unhealthy practice was still carried on by some Christians. Those with the most important jobs or roles would get preferred seating. James speaks out against this. It is our relationship with Christ that gives us dignity, not our profession or possessions.

The Christian answer is not reverse discrimination—treating the poor like royalty and the rich like scum. Our goal is to treat people without consideration for their status. No one is unworthy to be seated.

Once, as Jesus observed the behavior of people arriving for an important social event, he commented on the tendency to jostle for the places of honor (Luke 14:7-11). His instruction was, "But when you are invited, take the lowest place, so that when your host comes, he will say to you, 'Friend, move up to a better place.' Then you will be honored in the presence of all your fellow guests" (Luke 14:10 NIV). Jesus was warning against self-exaltation. Later, Jesus emphasized the danger of misreading outward evidence when he described how he appears to the world: "For I was hungry and you gave me something to eat, I was thirsty and you gave me something to drink, I was a stranger and you invited me in" (Matthew 25:35 NIV). The point is that favoritism is not just mistreating people or breaking a standard of conduct—it is, in fact, treating Jesus as though he had little value.

When we gather for worship, we ought to be conscious that even if we are familiar with everyone in the room, Christ is present. If there are two or three of us gathered in his name, he is there (Matthew 18:20). Before we worship, we ought to recognize Christ's presence. Can we not assume that he follows his own advice? When Jesus meets with us, does he assume a place of honor or jostle for our attention? Or should we imagine that Jesus takes the place of deepest humility among us and waits to be recognized as Lord? When we neglect or ignore the poor or powerless, we also ignore Christ.

2:4 Have you not discriminated among yourselves and become judges with evil thoughts?NIV James expected his readers to answer "yes" to his question. He condemned their behavior because Christ had made them all one. Paul later wrote, "There is no longer Jew or Greek, there is no longer slave or free, there is no longer male or female, for all of you are one in Christ Jesus" (Galatians 3:28 NRSV). These believers were ignoring that fact. They were forced to admit that they were discriminating against the poor person and becoming unjust judges with evil thoughts, making their judgments by worldly standards. As Christians they professed obedience to Christ, but their conduct defied him. Leviticus 19:15 firmly states: "Do not pervert justice; do not show partiality to the poor or favoritism to the great, but judge your neighbor fairly." In addition, they broke the commandment of Jesus, who said, "Judge not that you be not judged" (Matthew 7:1).

Why is it wrong to judge a person by his or her economic status? Wealth may indicate intelligence, wise decisions, and hard work. On the other hand, it may mean only that a person had the good fortune of being born into a wealthy family. Or it can even be a sign of greed, dishonesty, and selfishness. When we honor someone just because he or she dresses well, we make appearance more important than character. Sometimes we do this because:

- Poverty makes us uncomfortable, and we don't want to face our responsibilities to those who have less than we do.

- We too want to be wealthy, and we hope to use the rich person as a means to that end.

- We want the rich person to join our church and help support it financially.

All these motives are selfish. They may appear nothing more than practical considerations, but James calls them evil.

Another false assumption that sometimes influences our treatment of the rich is our misunderstanding of God's relationship to wealth. It is deceptively easy to believe riches are a sign of God's blessing and approval. But God does not promise us earthly rewards or riches; in fact, Christ calls us to be ready to suffer for him and give up everything in order to hold on to eternal life (Matthew 6:19-21; 19:28-30; Luke 12:14-34; 1 Timothy 6:17-19). We will have untold riches in eternity if we are faithful in our present life (Luke 6:35; John 12:23-25; Galatians 6:7-10; Titus 3:4-8).

2:5 **Has God not chosen the poor of this world to be rich in faith.** NKJV Jesus' first followers were common people. Christianity has a special message for the poor. Jesus often spoke of his mission to the poor: "Blessed are you poor, for yours is the kingdom of God" (Luke 6:20 NKJV; see also Matthew 11:5; Luke 4:18). In a social system that gave the poor very little, Jesus' message to them was certainly good news.

> God must love the common people because he made so many of them.
>
> *Abraham Lincoln*

Though most agree that James expected this rhetorical question to be answered "yes," some would argue that the biblical references to *poor* usually have to do with spiritual poverty. This is especially the case anytime the Bible seems to be saying that it might be an advantage to be poor. Their basis is the first Beatitude, "Blessed are the poor in spirit, for theirs is the kingdom of heaven" (Matthew 5:3 NKJV). It is fundamentally important for us to acknowledge our spiritual poverty before God. But here James is simply making the observation, and expecting us to agree, that the poor in spirit are most often the poor in material wealth.

WHO ARE THE POOR?
The poor are those who have little money and those whose simple values are despised by an affluent society like ours. Perhaps these "poor" people prefer serving rather than managing, human relationships rather than financial security, peace rather than power. The principle is not that the poor will automatically go to heaven and the rich to hell. Poor people, however, are usually more aware of their powerlessness. Thus it is often easier for them to acknowledge their need for salvation. One of the greatest barriers to salvation for the rich is pride. For the poor, bitterness can often bar the way. Don't allow plenty or poverty to keep you from God's gift of eternal life.

Elsewhere, Paul reminded believers of their humble roots: "Brothers, think of what you were when you were called. Not many of you were wise by human standards; not many were influential; not many were of noble birth" (1 Corinthians 1:26 NIV).

The poor people may not have mattered in that society, but they mattered very much to God. Each believer is very valuable to the church.

And to inherit the kingdom he promised those who love him?[NIV]

This does not mean that rich people are doomed and that poor people are automatically saved. Christianity offered much to the poor—the common people clamored to follow Jesus. But it demanded much of the rich. After speaking with Jesus, the rich young man "went away sad, because he had great wealth" (Matthew 19:22 NIV). The poverty of poor believers (those who love him) is only poverty in the eyes of the world, but they are rich in faith and will inherit the kingdom. The rich are not excluded from the kingdom; just as the poor are not "chosen" due to any merit of poverty. However, great riches can stand in the way of a person recognizing his or her need for God (Mark 10:23; Luke 12:34). The poor, on the other hand, have nothing about which they can boast before God (1 Corinthians 1:29). To continue to show favoritism to those who are only rich by the world's standards is not only wrong, but shortsighted.

Rich or poor, believers must obey God and love him. This could be called the heart of James's message. If we really love God, both our faith in him and our obedience to him will be right. We will not belittle anyone with whom we share a common inheritance.

2:6   But you have insulted the poor.[NIV] The Greek word for *insulted* is *etimasate*, which means "dishonored" (see NRSV; NKJV). James's readers had dishonored the poor because they did not treat them as God treats them. The vivid imagery of Jesus' parable of the unforgiving servant (Matthew 18:23-35) and his comment concerning the anointing given to him by the sinful woman (Luke 7:36-50) come to mind as the poor are being ignored or ushered to humble seats. Jesus' summary was, "Therefore, I tell you, her many sins have been forgiven—for she loved much. But he who has been forgiven little loves little" (Luke 7:47 NIV). None of us have been forgiven little. But we betray an attitude of pride when we treat each other without honor.

> To dishonor the poor is to dishonor those whom God honors, and so to invert the order of God.   *John Calvin*

James showed how evil their actions were by asking three questions.

Is it not the rich who are exploiting you?[NIV] In this society, the rich oppressed the poor. To *exploit* means to use someone for profit—to take advantage of someone and to use him or her self-ishly for one's own purposes. As we are reading these questions, we must remember James's original case study (2:2-4). Both the rich person and the poor person in mind here are probably visitors to the church who are unbelievers. At best they are people whose faith is not yet known. James's questions reveal his underlying observation that the believers are treating with great honor those they ought to approach with some reserve (the rich) because there is a high probability that they are not believers, while at the same time dishonoring those whom they ought to approach respectfully because, quite possibly, they are dealing with a brother or sister who is a believer, or who is quite likely to become one.

The rich exploiting the poor was not a new development; there are references to this throughout the Old Testament (Jeremiah 7:6; 22:3; Ezekiel 18:7; Amos 4:1; 8:4; Malachi 3:5). If a poor person needed a loan, the rich person might offer it, but often at exorbitant interest (even though charging interest to a fellow Israelite was forbidden by God's law—see Exodus 22:25). In first-century Palestine, landowners and merchants often accumulated wealth and power, forcing the poor people from the land and causing them to become even poorer.

Is it not they who drag you into court?[NIV] The rich typically showed no mercy or concern for the poor. They would take the poor to court, most likely for not repaying a debt. Wealthy moneylenders often took advantage of the poor. A creditor, if he met a debtor on the street, could literally grab him and drag him into court. James can ask this question because he takes it for granted that his readers would understand that believers are not to be taking legal action against each other. What an amazingly contemporary issue! What statement are we making to the world when it sees, within the church, believers habitually taking each other to court? The Bible does not deny that rightful grievances occur between people. But the options for settlement are broader and healthier. They include forgiveness, reconciliation, restitution—all handled among believers themselves (see, for example, Matthew 5:23-26; 1 Corinthians 6:1-8).

But economic persecution was not the only oppression these believers faced from the wealthy; James's third question focuses on religious persecution.

2:7 **Are they not the ones who are slandering the noble name of him to whom you belong?**[NIV] These rich people were abusing the name of Christ either by speaking evil of him or by insulting Christians. It hadn't taken long for the followers of Christ to be called Christians (*Christianous*) by those outside the church (Acts 11:26). Being identified with the name of Christ helped indicate that they belonged to him. To be called a "Christian" was not an honor; it was a reproach heaped upon the believers by unbelievers (see 1 Peter 4:13-14).

It often happens that those oppressed begin to act like their oppressors. How wrong that this should happen among believers. James pointed out the irony that Christians would show favoritism to those who were known to slander Christ!

James asks his readers to listen carefully while he reminds them of the role the rich tended to play in their society. They were oppressors who exploited the poor (2:6). The rich oppressed others by:

- Exploiting them and their livelihood (2:6)
- Threatening their security (2:6)
- Attacking their identity (2:7)

James's answer does not give us the option of retaliation. There is no room to say, "Get the rich before they get you." James's answer is, "Don't show favoritism." It is a negative application of the royal law that he is about to introduce, and upon which every application eventually rests.

2:8 If you really fulfill the royal law according to the Scripture, "You shall love your neighbor as yourself," you do well.NKJV Love is the source from which our attitudes toward others should flow. This *royal law* is a law from the king himself, in this case, the King of kings (see Matthew 22:37-40). This law is God's will for his followers, for he said, "Love each other as I have loved you" (John 15:12).

In the Old Testament (Leviticus 19:18; Proverbs 14:21), one's neighbor would be a fellow Israelite; but Jesus' application included everyone with whom we might come into contact—even foreigners (Luke 10:25-37) and enemies (Matthew 5:44). References by Jesus to Leviticus 19:18 are recorded six times in the Gospels. "Do not seek revenge or bear a grudge against one of your people, but love your neighbor as yourself. I am the Lord" (NIV, see Matthew 5:43; 7:12; 19:19; 22:37-40; Luke 6:31; 10:26-28). James was calling his readers to obey the royal law of love that would forbid them to discriminate against anyone who entered their fellowship.

We are to show favor to everyone, whether the person is rich or poor. We are to be kind, overlooking other superficial trappings. Our attitudes and actions toward others should be guided by love.

When asked what was the greatest commandment, Jesus replied, "'You shall love the Lord your God with all your heart, and with all your soul, and with all your mind.' . . . And . . . 'love your neighbor as yourself'" (Matthew 22:37-39 NRSV).

2:9 But if you show partiality, you commit sin and are convicted by the law as transgressors. NKJV James does not trivialize their actions. Showing favoritism is not a minor transgression or an unfortunate oversight; according to James it is sin, and those engaged in this action are lawbreakers. 1 John 3:4 says, "Everyone who sins breaks the law; in fact, sin is lawlessness" (NIV).

Discrimination against anyone, whether on the basis of dress, race, social class, wealth, sex, etc., is a clear violation of the royal law of love. We must treat all people as we would want to be treated. We should not ignore the rich because then we would be favoring them for what they can do for us, while ignoring the poor who can offer us little in return.

SHOWING FAVORITISM
Why is it wrong to show favoritism to the wealthy?

- It is inconsistent with Christ's teachings.
- It results from evil thoughts.
- It insults people made in God's image.
- It is a by-product of selfish motives.
- It goes against the biblical definition of love.
- It shows a lack of mercy to those less fortunate.
- It is hypocritical.
- It is sin.

2:10 For whoever shall keep the whole law, and yet stumble in one point, he is guilty of all. NKJV Even our attitudes and motives come under the law's jurisdiction. As Jesus explained in his Sermon on the Mount, "Anyone who is angry with his brother will be subject to judgment. . . . Anyone who looks at a woman lustfully has already committed adultery with her in his heart" (Matthew 5:22, 28 NIV). The attitude of favoritism was no different, so James points out to his readers that by their actions toward these wealthy visitors, they were actually breaking all of God's law.

Jesus said: "Anyone who breaks one of the least of these commandments and teaches others to do the same will be called least in the kingdom of heaven" (Matthew 5:19 NIV). The believers had not made the connection between God's command to love their neighbor and their discrimination against the poor. James's point here is not that showing favoritism is as "bad" as murder, but that no matter what commandment someone breaks, that person is guilty of an offense against God. He or she has violated the will of God. We cannot excuse the sin of favoritism by pointing to the rest of the good we do. Sin is not simply balanced against good—it must be confessed and forgiven.

So why is a person who commits one sin guilty of breaking them all? James is not attempting to discuss greater or lesser sins. He is pointing to the overall effect of any sin on our relationship with God. Where we tend to see God's rules like a fabric, James sees glass. If we throw a small or large stone at the fabric, the hole will be similar in shape and size to the rock thrown. If we throw a stone at the glass, however, any sized stone will shatter the glass. This does not mean that breaking any commandment is just as bad as breaking any other (for example, stealing bread instead of murdering a person). It does mean that deliberately breaking any commandment shows our attitude toward God's direction for our life.

> A person may observe all the laws of health, but if he inhales one whiff of poison, he may die; so we may be outwardly obedient to the entire Decalogue, but delinquency in love will invalidate everything.   *F. B. Meyer*

Christians must not use this verse to justify sinning. We dare not say: "Because I can't keep every demand of God, why even try?" James reminds us that if we've broken just one law, we are sinners. We can't decide to keep part of God's law and ignore the rest. We can't break the law a little bit. If we have broken it at all, we need Christ's payment for our sin. We must measure ourselves, not anyone else, against God's standards. Once we have asked for forgiveness for our sins, we must renew our efforts to put our faith into practice each day.

2:11 For He who said, "Do not commit adultery," also said, "Do not murder." Now if you do not commit adultery, but you do murder, you have become a transgressor of the law.NKJV Here James illustrates his point that the law is a unit, and to break one law is to become guilty of the entire law. Jewish theologians of the day would have disagreed with James, saying some laws were "light" and some "heavy," meaning that breaking some was not as serious as breaking others. It might seem that stumbling on the act of showing favoritism is breaking one of those "least commandments," not nearly as bad as committing adultery or murdering. But God's law was not written with "heavy" and "light" commands so that obedience to some outweighed obedience to others. Believers are called to consistent obedience.

From our perspective, there do seem to be degrees of sin. The immediate effects of some sins seem much more destructive and horrible than others. This is true. What we must remember, however, is God's perspective. He not only sees immediate effects, but he also sees hidden and long-term effects. And the long-term effect of all sin is rebellion against God. We make a serious error when we get caught up in discussing possible degrees of sin. It is as if we persist in asking God the question, "How badly must I sin before the law is broken?" Whereas the question we ought to be asking is, "Have I grasped the truth that any sin, no matter how insignificant it may seem to me, shatters the law?"

By the time Nathan confronted David about his relationship with Bathsheba, David had managed to break most of the commandments (see 2 Samuel 11:1–12:23). Among other things, David had disobeyed God, coveted another man's wife, stolen her, plotted the man's murder, and lied repeatedly. Psalm 51 records David's repentant desire for forgiveness: "Against you, you only, have I sinned and done what is evil in your sight, so that you are proved right when you speak and justified when you judge" (Psalm 51:4 NIV). Before God, self-justification is always a wasted effort. As lawbreakers we should come in confession and humility, placing ourselves under God's mercy and grace.

2:12 Speak and act as those who are going to be judged by the law that gives freedom. NIV Obedience must also be a lifestyle, a habit. *Speak and act* covers all human behavior (see also Acts 1:1; 7:22; 1 John 3:18).

The believers would be judged on the basis of their obedience to God's will as expressed in his law. Although God has accepted those who believe in him, we are still called upon to obey him. But his law is not a burden; instead, it *gives freedom* because we are obeying out of joy. We are grateful that God has given us freedom from sin's penalty and the Spirit to empower us to do his will. Peter adds the special caution, "Live as free men, but do not use your freedom as a cover-up for evil; live as servants of God" (1 Peter 2:16).

The specific command is to speak and act as believers. The command implies *chosen* behavior. Christians can be held responsible by the world for our bad example. Nothing is sadder than believers whose words and actions demonstrate that they are still under the influence of the world rather than under the influence of Christ. One of the basic rights we give to Christ when we surrender to his lordship is the right to speak as we want to speak and act as we want to act. Those choices now must be made under Christ's direction. The freedom we experience in Christ is the by-product of living the way God designed us. There can be no doubt that Jesus had this in mind when he said, "By this all men will know that you are my disciples, if you love one another" (John 13:35).

Without verses 12 and 13, this paragraph would appear little different than the crushing system that many of these Jewish Christians had lived under all their lives: the constant reminders of the demands of the law; the details of keeping the ceremonial laws; the threat of ostracism for overlooking some detail in the tradition; the power of religious figures to control people's lives. In these two verses, James points out once again the radical nature of the Christian message.

Those who are suspicious of James's references to the law must account for the way Jesus himself treated the law. He said, "Do not think that I have come to abolish the Law or the Prophets; I have not come to abolish them but to fulfill them" (Matthew 5:17). We can actually say that Jesus did not come to lead people out from under the law, but rather to help them fulfill it. He found them lost and gave them the way home. Our resistance to the idea of law is partly and rightly based on the horror of legalism and what it has done throughout history. But our resistance is also based on a misunderstanding of the law and of grace. Without the law of God, there is no grace. If we remove God's holy standard that holds us accountable and directs our lives, we have removed at the same time the framework in which grace operates. To paraphrase the apostle Paul (see Romans 5:20-21), the law shows us how much sin abounds; and it isn't until we see how much sin abounds that we are able to see that grace abounds even more!

Jesus confronted a religious system that had annulled or trivialized God's standards. There was no need for grace because God's standards had been translated into "things that determined people could accomplish with a great deal of effort." Divine purity and perfection had been redefined into human self-righteousness and superficial rule-keeping. Jesus reintroduced the world to the awesome character of God: holy, just, and gracious. The Incarnation was not a revision or change in God's eternal plan—it was God's plan brought to fulfillment.

As Christians, we are saved by God's free gift (grace) through faith, not by keeping the law. But as Christians, we are also required to obey Christ. The apostle Paul taught, "For all of us must appear before the judgment seat of Christ" (2 Corinthians 5:10 NRSV) to be judged for our conduct. God's grace does not cancel our duty to obey him; it gives our obedience a new basis. The law is no longer an external set of rules, but it is a law that gives freedom—one that we joyfully and willingly carry out because we love God and because we have the power of his Holy Spirit to carry it out (see 1:25).

2:13 Because judgment without mercy will be shown to anyone who has not been merciful. NIV Mercy is precisely what the believers were *not* showing when they insulted poor people. If they continued to discriminate, they would be in danger of facing their own judgment without mercy. This is an excellent statement of New Testament ethics: What we do to others we actually do to God, and he returns it upon our heads.

The relationship between mercy and concern for the poor is made clear in Zechariah 7:9-10: "This is what the LORD Almighty says: 'Administer true justice; show mercy and compassion to one another. Do not oppress the widow or the fatherless, the alien or the poor: In your hearts do not think evil of each other'" (NIV, see also Isaiah 58:7-9).

We must be merciful because God is merciful:

- "The LORD, the LORD, the compassionate and gracious God, slow to anger, abounding in love and faithfulness" (Exodus 34:6 NIV).

- "Because the LORD your God is a merciful God" (Deuteronomy 4:31 NRSV).

- "The LORD is compassionate and gracious, slow to anger, abounding in love. . . . As a father has compassion on his children, so the LORD has compassion on those who fear him" (Psalm 103:8, 13 NIV).

But Jesus made it clear that God will show mercy only to those who do likewise (see Matthew 5:7; 6:14-15; 12:7; 18:21-35; 25:31-46; Mark 11:25). We stand before God in need of his mercy. We can't earn forgiveness by forgiving others. But when we withhold forgiveness from others after having received it ourselves, we show that we don't understand or appreciate God's mercy toward us.

Mercy triumphs over judgment! Not showing mercy places us only under the judgment of God, but showing mercy places us under God's mercy as well as his judgment. We will always deserve God's judgment because we can never adequately obey God's royal law. But our merciful actions are evidence of our relationship with Christ. And it is that relationship that vindicates

57

us. We stand before God, from whom we know we deserve judgment and upon whom we are depending for mercy. Because of God's character, his mercy triumphs over judgment.

VITAL FAITH LEADS US TO DEMONSTRATE MERCY

If we have vital faith we will:

- not express hasty criticisms of our church leaders or pastors
- not be so demanding in our expectations of our spouse
- show more tolerance with others whose habits or manners irritate us
- show greater patience with those who learn slowly and with those who simply seem to have more difficulties in life
- treat others with the same kindness, generosity, compassion, and understanding that we long to experience ourselves

The world is looking for evidence that God is merciful. Being people who have experienced mercy and who express mercy will catch their attention.

FAITH RESULTS IN GOOD WORKS / 2:14-26

The remainder of chapter 2 is often cited to show that the teachings of James and Paul were completely contradictory.

- James: *"Faith without works is dead"* (2:26 NKJV).
- Paul: *"For we maintain that a man is justified by faith apart from observing the law"* (Romans 3:28 NIV); *"A person is justified not by the works of the law, but through faith in Jesus Christ"* (Galatians 2:16 NRSV).

However, careful reading and understanding of both Paul and James will show that instead of contradicting, their writings really complement each other.

First, consider the writers' viewpoints in light of the situations they were addressing in their letters. They were confronting different issues. Paul was responding to the Judaizers, who said works—such as circumcision and observing Jewish ceremonial laws—were necessary for salvation. James was responding to those who believed that mere intellectual agreement was enough to obtain salvation.

Second, there is a difference in the time frame in the believer's life as they make their statements. Paul began at the very beginning—at conversion. No one can ever *earn* God's forgiveness and salvation. We can only accept it. James spoke to the professing believer, one who has already accepted that forgiveness and salvation, explaining that the person must live a new life. No one can be saved by works; no one can be saved without producing works. We are not saved *by* good works, but *for* good works. James's point was not that works must be added to faith, but that genuine faith includes works.

THREE PRINCIPLES OF FAITH

In chapter 2, James argues against favoritism and for the necessity of good deeds. He presents three principles of faith:

1. Commitment is an essential part of faith. You cannot be a Christian simply by affirming the right doctrines, agreeing with the biblical facts, or even giving mental assent to the gospel (2:19). You must commit your mind and heart to Christ.
2. Right actions are the natural by-products of true faith. A genuine Christian will have a changed life (2:18). The gospel is a seed that will eventually prove its vitality by its fruit.
3. Faith without good works doesn't do anyone any good—it is useless and perhaps lifeless (2:14-17). If a planted seed never sends up a shoot and never ripens, how can someone claim it took root?

James's teachings are consistent with Paul's teaching that we receive salvation by faith alone. Paul emphasized the purpose of faith—to bring salvation. James emphasized the results of faith—a changed life.

Each of us stands before the challenges of Paul and James. They were human vehicles for God's Word. If we have not yet heard Paul's message of salvation by grace through faith, it is here that we must start. If we have accepted God's offer of salvation and are claiming Jesus Christ as Lord and Savior we must listen to James's challenge to live out that faith in obedience. One message communicates the required foundation; the other directs a lifelong building project.

2:14 What good is it . . . if you say you have faith but do not have works?NRSV The man who claims to have faith obviously thinks that his belief alone, without any good deeds (actions done in obedience to God), is satisfactory in God's sight. He need not be concerned about anyone else.

However, talk is cheap, and so unsubstantiated claims are worthless. Faith not accompanied by deeds has no saving value. Anyone can say he has faith, but if his lifestyle remains selfish and worldly, then what good is that faith? It is merely faith that believes *about* Jesus, not faith that believes *in* him.

Can faith save you? NRSV No, it cannot. The structure of the Greek for this question expects a negative answer. The faith that saves is faith that proves itself in the actions it produces.

GOOD WORKS IN THE NEW TESTAMENT

John the Baptist—His message emphasized repentance. John encouraged people to demonstrate their repentance through baptism, but he did not make the symbol a substitute for obedience (see Matthew 3:1-12; Luke 3:1-18). John issued a general standard, "Produce fruit in keeping with repentance" (Luke 3:8 NIV), but followed that with specific applications for those who asked: to the crowd, "The man with two tunics should share with him who has none, and the one who has food should do the same" (Luke 3:11 NIV); to the tax collectors, "Don't collect any more than you are required to" (Luke 3:13 NIV); to the soldiers, "Don't extort money and don't accuse people falsely—be content with your pay" (Luke 3:14 NIV).

Jesus—Jesus never left the impression that following him was an exercise in blind faith without actions (see Matthew 7:15-27). In fact, his standard was sobering: "For I tell you that unless your righteousness surpasses that of the Pharisees and the teachers of the law, you will certainly not enter the kingdom of heaven" (Matthew 5:20). Jesus also made it clear, however, that "works" were no substitute for faith. When people were healed, for instance, it was by faith (see Mark 5:34). He stated very clearly the order of events: "I tell you the truth, anyone who has faith in me will do what I have been doing. He will do even greater things than these, because I am going to the Father" (John 14:12 NIV).

Paul—The apostle of faith had much to say about works, and not all of it was negative. Paul's order was identical to Christ's: faith must come before works, but genuine faith always leads to works of obedience (see Romans 2:6-11; 13:12-14; 14:12; 2 Corinthians 5:6-10; Galatians 6:2-10; Ephesians 2:8-10; Colossians 3:1-10). Paul made it clear that we are saved by grace through faith, but with an expected result: "For it is by grace you have been saved, through faith—and this not from yourselves, it is the gift of God—not by works, so that no one can boast. For we are God's workmanship, created in Christ Jesus to do good works, which God prepared in advance for us to do" (Ephesians 2:8-10 NIV). We are not saved by works, but we are saved to do good works.

Two images help us remember the importance of genuine faith:

1. On one side are people who project confidence in their standing before God and yet show no evidence that their faith affects any of their actions. They may even take pride in the fact that they can believe what they want and that no one has

the right to challenge their faith. After all, "only God really knows for sure," they may say.

We can agree that allowing oneself to be forced to prove something can, at times, actually be evidence that we are not sure ourselves. For instance, when Jesus was tempted by Satan in the wilderness (Matthew 4:1-11; Mark 1:12-13; Luke 4:1-13), he was challenged to prove he was the Son of God. The proof was easily within Jesus' ability. Yet Jesus rejected the challenge because trying to "prove" he was the Son of God would have subjected him to the influence of Satan. If Jesus had felt compelled to prove his divinity, that feeling would have betrayed self-doubt. Jesus did not doubt his identity—he demonstrated who he was many times, but not at the whim of others. Similarly, we must not attempt to demonstrate faith "on cue," or at the command of others, but our faith must still result in action.

2. On the other side are people whose lives demonstrate such a frantic flurry of activity that they literally have no time to need.

JAMES AND PAUL ON FAITH AND WORKS

James and Paul each meant something different in using the words *faith* and *works*. Each of them was responding to a different need.

	James	*Paul*
FAITH	Concerned with the danger of "dead faith"—he knew that shallow beliefs would never stand up to the trials believers would face in life. People will claim faith, but an unsubstantiated claim may be only empty words (see James 2:14).	Concerned with the exercise of "true faith," or saving faith—this faith not only opens the door for grace, but leads to obedient action (see Ephesians 2:8-10).
WORKS	Claims works are the natural product of faith that is alive—he emphasized the post-salvation results of the life of faith. This is very similar to Ephesians 2:8-10.	Calls "works" those legalistic efforts to secure one's own salvation—any attempt at self-justification was called works. For Paul, the beginning of salvation was always faith. After that, works followed (see Galatians 3:2).

think or talk about their faith. Those people, whose lives at first exhibit the marks of someone who believes, turn out to have real doubts. They doubt God's acceptance and feel compelled to work very hard in hopes of gaining that acceptance. But trying hard to build merit with God becomes a substitute for faith. We first come to God by faith, receiving what we could never hope to earn. Then, out of gratitude, we seek to serve the One who loves us in every way we possibly can. Our faith leads to grateful work.

James helps us see that genuine faith will always combine deep trust in God and consistent action in the world. It is not the one who claims to have faith, but the one who actually has faith who is saved.

Someone may ask, "But what if genuine belief never really gets a chance to demonstrate itself in action?" We answer by saying first that God sees genuine belief long before it is apparent to us. After all, James's discussion is not intended to be used to sift the faith of others, but rather as a tool to weigh our own faith. James is telling us that, given enough time, faith will demonstrate its liveliness by action. One instance of genuine faith given little time is the case of the thief on the cross who believed in Jesus (Luke 23:32-43). In sight of death, this man ackowledged Jesus as the Christ. One man, no longer able to do anything but trust, believed in the one who was doing his greatest work on a cross. The thief truly believed yet was able to do no "works" . . . or was he? Did even this man's short-lived, genuine faith lead to real action? Certainly it did! The apostle Paul clearly describes what is probably the first "work" most believers do when their faith is genuine: they verbally confess their faith (see Romans 10:9-10). The dying thief said a few words of profound eloquence: "Jesus, remember me when you come into your kingdom" (Luke 23:42 NRSV). The thief could not possibly have known how many times his simple trusting witness during his final agony would give hope to others who felt they were beyond God's help.

Most of us have a great deal more time than the thief on the cross. Does our life count for as much? Do we declare our faith and then demonstrate its vitality throughout our life?

2:15 Suppose a brother or sister is without clothes and daily food.[NIV] This hypothetical person may have been someone in the church fellowship—a brother or sister—who was in real need. To be without clothing and food is to be in a desperate yet all-too-common situation. James's second case study also rings true in contemporary life. There is hardly a church today within whose walls there are not persons who live without adequate food and shelter.

The problem of world hunger is greater than most of us can visualize or respond to, so we often fail to help the problem. But James invites us to think of *a brother or sister;* not all the poor in town, or all the hungry in the state. Working towards those huge needs begins within reach, with someone in our own fellowship. People are fed and clothed one at a time.

2:16 **One of you says to him.** James leaves no doubt that the person in need is a brother or sister in Christ. The argument is strikingly similar to John's words: "If anyone has material possessions and sees his brother in need but has no pity on him, how can the love of God be in him? Dear children, let us not love with words or tongue but with actions and in truth" (1 John 3:17-18 NIV).

"Go, I wish you well."NIV This reflects a standard farewell blessing in Hebrew. The emphasis is on *Go!* It implied that the departing friend's present needs were met and that one was hoping for the same in the future.

"Keep warm and well fed."NIV The idea here is that the well-wisher is saying, "Please go, and may God take care of you because I don't have the time." This brings out the hypocrisy of those who, in a sense, are asking God to do what God wants *them* to do. Also, one of the key elements of prayer, as in Matthew 9:35-38, followed by the mission in Matthew 10, is that when we pray for God to do something there is a very real chance that we may be the ones to fulfill our own prayer request, and God demands that we consider that possibility.

But does nothing about his physical needs, what good is it?NIV Something could be done for this person. There would be plenty of clothes and food in the fellowship to care for this person, but the person was sent away empty-handed, with a prayer over his head, but no clothing on his back or food in his stomach.

Too often, we in the church offer mere words—prayers, advice, encouragement—when we are being called upon to act. The need is obvious, and the resources are not lacking, yet the help is not given. Faith that does not result in actions is no more effective than a pious wish for the poor person to be warmed and fed—the wish accomplishes nothing. Among Paul's final words to the Galatians were, "Therefore, as we have opportunity, let us do good to all people, especially to those who belong to the family of believers" (Galatians 6:10 NIV). James is describing Christians who miss the opportunities to help.

WHAT ABOUT PHYSICAL NEEDS?
Have we received God's gracious gifts and yet withheld them from others? Here are some ways we can give:

- Look for a single parent in need of help—car repairs, child care, help with financial or legal concerns.
- Provide meals for a sick or grieving family.
- Help a student whose college finances are a burden.
- Assist a young family with clothes and toys for the children.
- Help a young couple facing stress by funding a retreat or vacation for them.

2:17 **In the same way, faith by itself, if it is not accompanied by action, is dead.**^{NIV} A conviction or intellectual belief that refuses to obey the commands of Christ is unprofitable—it is dead. *Action* is the fruit of living faith. If there are no positive actions, then the professed faith is dead. The right actions prove our faith to be real faith.

We might call this approach by James an argument from compassion. He is taking for granted the truth that spoken help is not adequate when material help is required. Real compassion doesn't just talk; it does. In the same way, writes James, faith is not just a matter of saying the right words—it must also be accompanied by action. Believing involves keeping company with action. If those around us note our actions, they should be led to know the faith that motivates them. If others hear us speak of faith, they must also see us act out that faith. The emphasis is on both: our life representing a genuine fellowship of faith and action. The balance can be kept by asking ourselves two questions regularly: (1) to whom should I explain why I live the way I do? and (2) who needs to see more clearly that I back up my words of faith with action?

2:18 **But someone will say, "You have faith and I have works."**^{NRSV} This *someone* may have been someone James personally knew, but it seems more likely that this was a hypothetical person who poses an argument to James. This someone considers faith and works to be separate and alternate expressions of Christianity. "You do your deeds, I'll have my faith, and we'll be religious in our own ways." But the two cannot be separated without ceasing to be alive. Faith lives in the action it generates; actions require faith to gain a particular meaning.

Show me your faith without your works, and I will show you my faith by my works.^{NKJV} James responded with a challenge: Show me your faith without deeds. It cannot be done! Faith cannot be demonstrated apart from action. Faith is within us; it can only be seen by the actions it produces through us. Anyone can profess faith, but only action shows its genuineness.

The "self-styled religion" mentality that is such a part of today's world needs to be challenged with as much vigor as James challenged the mistake in his own time. Any faith that does not move its believers to action is a faith not worth holding. Any believer who is not moved by his faith has a weak hold on what he claims to believe. And actions that are not expressions of faith rooted in the grace of Jesus Christ are pointless efforts.

2:19 You believe that there is one God. You do well. Even the demons believe—and tremble. NKJV That God is one was a basic teaching of Judaism: "Hear, O Israel: The Lord our God, the Lord is one" (Deuteronomy 6:4 NIV—known as the *Shema*). The Jews were well known for their ardent monotheism. It was even a source of national pride in a world characterized by polytheism. Israel was confident that she had been given the revelation of God, and he was one. But James points out that acceptance of a creed (even a true one) is not enough to save anyone. The demons have complete and thorough conviction that there is one God, but they are terrified by that truth. They believe in God only to hate and resist him in every way they can. Their "faith" even moves them to a negative reaction, while the faith of some of James's readers isn't real enough to give them a shiver. The demons shudder (an expression of fear, revulsion, and hatred) and demonstrate that their "faith" is real, though misdirected.

Mere assent to the existence of God often leads only to ignoring or fearing him. Believing that *anything* or anyone exists does not bring us into right relationship with them. It is not satisfying progress for a wife who has been ignored to have her husband suddenly announce that he now admits she exists. The movement might be in the right direction, but it is hardly noticeable. Likewise, we have not impressed God by grudgingly admitting his existence. At that point, we share the uncomfortable position of being even with God's enemies. Saving faith, then, is not merely intellectual agreement. It starts deep within us and expresses itself through our actions.

> The devil hath no promise, therefore he is excluded from Paul's faith. The devil believeth that Christ died, but not that he died for his sins.
>
> *William Tyndale, on comparing James and Paul*

Almost all Christian traditions include making *vows* before God and repeating the historic creeds of the church. But it is not unusual to find adults who admit that they affirmed baptismal or membership vows without ever giving serious thought to what they were actually saying. They describe themselves as simply nodding their heads at the appropriate time while trusting the clergy to say the right words. Others can say the Apostles' Creed in one breath without mentally interacting with a single word they have uttered. It is this kind of thoughtless, actionless, lifeless faith that James repeatedly challenges. He is not contending that believing in one God is trite. What he is urging us to do is to express, with our actions, the kind of life that ought to characterize someone who knows God. He is challenging us with applications of Jesus' words: "'Love the Lord your God with all your heart and with all your soul and with all your mind.' This is the first and greatest commandment. And the second is like it: 'Love your neighbor as yourself'" (Matthew 22:37-39 NIV).

2:20 You senseless person. ^NRSV James again addresses his hypothetical person. This style was a customary feature of ancient apologetic documents (see also Matthew 23:17; Luke 24:25; Romans 2:1; 9:20; 1 Corinthians 15:36; Galatians 3:1). James is not addressing anyone in particular. It is an excellent way, however, to force personal application. The point of the argument is directed back to the reader.

The foolish person is literally a "hollow man" *(anthrope kene)*. If the faith around which we build our lives turns out to be empty, we are truly hollow people.

Do you want to be shown . . . that faith apart from works is barren? ^NRSV James prepares to show from the Scriptures that real faith always has works. The phrase here is literally, "But are you willing to know?"—indicating that he realizes the problem may reside in his readers' will rather than in their having good reasons to act upon their faith. There are times when we need more teaching or understanding in order to respond to God's direction. But most often we know what needs to be done, yet are unwilling to act. When it comes to putting into practice what we know, is it our habit to obey God?

From his own case studies, James now turns to historical figures from the Old Testament that he expects will confirm what he has been teaching about the importance of active faith.

2:21 Was not our ancestor Abraham justified by works when he offered his son Isaac on the altar? ^NKJV Abraham was one of the Old Testament figures most revered by the Jews (see Genesis

TWELVE TESTS OF ABRAHAM

Abraham's faith was tested at least twelve specific times. Some of them were not what we might call big tests, but together they establish a picture of Abraham as a person whose faith was genuine. After the last of these, God said, "Now I know that you fear God, because you have not withheld from me your son, your only son" (Genesis 22:12).

Each of Abraham's tests can have applications for us:

Reference	Test	Application
Genesis 12:1-7	Abraham left Ur and Haran for an unknown destination at God's direction.	Do I trust God with my future? Is his will part of my decision making?
Genesis 13:8-13	Abraham directed a peaceful separation from Lot and settled at the oaks of Mamre.	Do I trust God with my interests even when I seem to be receiving an unfair settlement?
Genesis 14:13-16	Abraham rescued Lot from the five kings.	Does my faithfulness to others bear witness to my trust in God's faithfulness?
Genesis 14:17-24	Abraham gave a tithe of loot to the godly king of Salem, Melchizedek, and refused the gift of the king of Sodom.	Am I watchful in my dealings with people that I give proper honor to God and refuse to receive honor that belongs to him?
Genesis 15:1-6	Abraham trusted God's promise that he would have a son.	How often do I consciously reaffirm my trust in God's promises?
Genesis 15:7-11	Abraham received the promised land by faith, though the fulfillment would not come for many generations.	How have I demonstrated my continued trust in God during those times when I have been required to wait?
Genesis 17:9-27	At God's command, Abraham circumcised every male in his family.	In what occasions in my life have I acted simply in obedience to God, and not because I understood the significance of what I was doing?

Reference	Test	Application
Genesis 18:1-8	Abraham welcomed strangers, who turned out to be angels.	When was the last time I practiced hospitality?
Genesis 18:22-33	Abraham prayed for Sodom.	Am I eager to see people punished, or do I care for people in spite of their sinfulness?
Genesis 20:1-17	Abraham admitted to wrongdoing and took the actions needed to set things right.	When I sin, is my tendency to cover up, or confess? Do I practice the truth that an apology must sometimes be accompanied by restitution?
Genesis 21:22-34	Abraham negotiated a treaty with Abimelech concerning a well.	Can people depend on my words and promises?
Genesis 22:1-12	Abraham prepared to sacrifice his son Isaac.	In what ways has my life demonstrated that I will not allow anything to come before God?

11:27–25:11 for Abraham's biography). Abraham's remarkable obedience in being willing to sacrifice his son at God's command was evidence of the works for which Abraham was called righteous.

What *was* Abraham doing when he offered his son Isaac on the altar? He was trusting God. The lesson we can draw from Abraham's life is not a comparison between his sacrifices and ours. We can expect that in one way or another, our faith will have to grow from internal trust to external action. Eventually, like Abraham, we too will have to answer the question, "Do I really trust God?"

2:22 Faith was active along with works.^{NRSV} Abraham had great faith in God (Genesis 15:6), but James points out that Abraham's faith was much more than just belief in the one God—the fruit of Abraham's great faith was in his deeds.

Faith was brought to completion by the works.^{NRSV} The Greek here has a play on words: Abraham's faith was working (*sunergei*) with his works (*ergois*). His faith produced his works, and his works completed his faith, meaning they "perfected" or "matured" it. Mature and complete believers (1:4) are produced through perseverance in trials; mature and complete faith is produced through works of obedience to God. Faith and works should not be confused with each other, but neither can they be separated from each other.

2:23 **"Abraham believed God, and it was accounted to him as righteousness."**NKJV Abraham believed God, so God gave Abraham the status of a right relationship with him—and this happened *before* Abraham's noted works (such as his willingness to sacrifice Isaac), and even before Abraham was circumcised (see Paul's words in Romans 4:1-17). But Abraham's faith and God's response *fulfilled* Scripture (meaning "filled" or "filled up"—gave their complete significance) when Abraham "completed" his faith by what he did (2:22). The Scripture to which James is referring is Genesis 15:6. Paul emphasized the chronology of Abraham's life, pointing out that he was called righteous before his noted works. James showed that Abraham's righteousness was the basis and reason for all those works.

He was called the friend of God.NRSV Because of Abraham's great faith and obedience, he held the privileged status of God's friend (see also 2 Chronicles 20:7; Isaiah 41:8). The word *friend* (*philos*) is the same one Jesus used in John 15:14. There Jesus stated that an ingredient of friendship is obedience: "You are my friends if you do what I command you" (John 15:14 NRSV). Among Jesus' commands earlier during that occasion was this: "Do not let your hearts be troubled. Trust in God; trust also in me" (John 14:1 NIV). Acting out our trust in God will lead to friendship with him, as it did in Abraham's case.

2:24 **You see that a person is justified by works and not by faith alone.**NRSV Many have said that this statement contradicts Paul's position, who wrote: "For we maintain that a man is justified by faith apart from observing the law" (Romans 3:28 NIV). Indeed, if both James and Paul used the word *justified* in the same way, this verse would contradict Paul's teaching about justification by faith alone. But for James, *justified* refers to God's final verdict over our entire Christian life, whereby we are declared righteous for having lived a life that was faithful to the end. For Paul, justified is the initial granting of righteousness upon a person's acceptance of Christ. For James, "works" (what he does) are the natural products of true faith; for Paul, "works" (observing the law) are what people were trying to *do* in order to be saved. For James, faith alone is the shallow belief in an idea; no commitment or life change is involved. For Paul, faith is saving faith—the belief that brings about an intimate union with Christ and results in salvation *and* obedience.

Paul made clear that a person enters into God's kingdom only by faith; James made clear that God requires good deeds from those who *are* "in" the kingdom.

A person receives salvation by faith alone, not by doing works of obedience; but a saved person does works of obedience because of that faith. For people who rely on their religious "busyness" for their salvation or merit before God, Paul's words are critical—those works alone can do nothing to save them. For people who rely on their intellectual assent of a belief, with only a verbal commitment, James's words are critical—their belief alone can do nothing to save them.

Two brief questions that help us monitor our spiritual health are: Who am I trusting? and Why am I working? If we are trusting anyone (including ourselves) other than Christ as the source and provider of our justification, we are lost. If we are acting for any reason other than in obedience and thanksgiving to Christ for what he has done for us, we are lost. We only truly find our salvation in Christ. Out of our trust in him will flow action.

2:25 In the same way, was not even Rahab the prostitute considered righteous for what she did when she gave lodging to the spies and sent them off in a different direction?NIV God's final judgment on a person's life considers the righteousness that person shows through works. But why would James bring up Rahab? After speaking of the great faith of Abraham, the father of Israel, James cited the example of Rahab, a pagan woman with a bad reputation (see Joshua 2:1-24; 6:22-25). But these two people, as opposite as they were, cemented James's argument—both people were declared righteous on the basis of their works that resulted from their faith. The contrast is not between faith and works, but between genuine faith and false faith.

If Abraham had not had faith, he would not have followed God. If Rahab had not had faith, she would never have decided to side with Israel—"For the LORD your God is God in heaven above and on the earth below" (Rahab's words in Joshua 2:11 NIV).

Yet if Abraham had not been willing to obey God, his faith would have meant nothing. If Rahab had not risked her life to help the spies, her faith would have accomplished nothing. But she is listed in the Hall of Faith in Hebrews: "By faith the prostitute Rahab, because she welcomed the spies, was not killed with those who were disobedient" (Hebrews 11:31 NIV).

Many have pointed out that Abraham and Rahab could represent opposite extremes of society. James may have used them for that reason, but they were also his relatives—Abraham in a general way as father of the Jewish nation, and Rahab in a specific way as one of the ancestors of David, Jesus Christ, and James (see Matthew 1:5). Both these heroes demonstrate the fact that real faith can survive in people with "feet of clay." The Bible describes neither Abraham nor Rahab as perfect. In fact, the spotlight shines on their sins as much as on their trust. Both demonstrated in their own way a tendency to lie (see Genesis 20:1-2; Joshua 2:3-7). Neither could have pointed to a life of perfect obedience as the reason for God's acceptance. Rather, each pointed to a life that illustrated their need for God and their trust in God.

2:26 As it is, the body without the spirit is dead, so faith without deeds is dead. Faith and deeds are as important to each other as body and spirit. Deeds are not added to faith; instead, the right kind of faith is faith that "works," that results in good deeds. Otherwise, Christianity is nothing more than an idea.

No one is moved to action without faith; no one's faith is real unless it moves him or her to action. The action is obedience to God. This draws us back to James's words in the first part of this chapter concerning care for others. The believer must do what God calls him to do—serve his brothers and sisters in Christ, refuse to discriminate among them, and help them out with good deeds.

Understanding how faith and deeds work together still doesn't mean that our life will be different. James is about to continue with a series of life situations that we all encounter. It is in these everyday events that we demonstrate our faith to be alive or dead. From time to time, we need to take our own spiritual pulse by matching our life with God's Word. But we also need to have people around us, the body of Christ, whom we can ask, "How do you see me putting my faith in Christ into action?"

O it is a living, busy active mighty thing, this faith. It is impossible for it not to be doing good things incessantly. It does not ask whether good works are to be done, but before the question is asked, it has already done this, and is constantly doing them. Whoever does not do such works, however, is an unbeliever. He gropes and looks around for faith and good works, but knows neither what faith is nor what good works are. Yet he talks and talks, with many words, about faith and good works.   *Martin Luther*

James 3

In this chapter, James's immediate concern is with the speech of false teachers who are ruining believers with their uncontrolled tongues. From that immediate concern he launches into the wider area of the use of speech among believers.

In the early church, teachers were very important. Both the survival and spiritual depth of believers depended on them. In the church at Antioch, they were ranked in status with the prophets who sent out Paul and Barnabas (Acts 13:1). Teachers were the point of contact for all new believers because converts needed instruction in the facts of the gospel, and teachers would build them up in the faith. The problem, however, was that some teachers had the ability to communicate but were driven by very worldly motivations. They would take leading positions in a church, form cliques, and use their teaching positions to criticize others. In this way, they could maintain their position and importance.

Chapter 3 is an elaboration of 1:19, "slow to speak." Christians need constant diligence and discipline. Nowhere is this more necessary than in the use of the tongue. Christians need help from God to speak wisely. All believers should take this chapter to heart, not just leaders and teachers; all Christians need to control what they say. And all types of speech, private and public, need to be brought under Christ's control. The only sure cure for selfishly motivated teaching and speaking is true repentance. This involves being honest and humble before God and admitting our sins (4:6-10). Only then will we be able to avoid sinful speech and bring healing to the Christian community.

3:1 **Not many of you should presume to be teachers.**[NIV] James taught that people should not rush to be teachers. Many of his status-conscious readers would have desired the reputable position of teachers in the community.

What was so attractive about being a teacher? Becoming a rabbi or teacher was the highest calling of a Jewish child.

Teachers had great influence and status in the early church (Ephesians 4:11). Because teachers were rare, each teacher had much work to do, and teaching was central to the work of the church. Because teachers taught primarily through verbal communication, it was vital for them to control what they said. Through their positions, teachers could present wrong doctrine. They could also create divisions in the church by promoting themselves rather than the message of Christ.

That some will presume they are teachers is implied but not actually stated by the text. Coming hard on the heels of chapter 2, one of the most honorable "works" that would immediately come to the Jewish mind would be the position of teaching. James has in mind a greater emphasis on spiritual growth and self-control before someone assumed the role of a teacher.

We who teach will be judged with greater strictness. NRSV
Teachers will have the greater judgment. Teaching authority carries with it greater responsibility. As works reveal the depths of a person's faith, so words show the depth of a person's maturity. The teacher is held to greater accountability because of his or her key teaching role (Luke 12:42-48). James is not against teachers; instead, he is alerting us to the great responsibilities that go with teaching and its potential problems. James valued the ministry of teaching, but he knew that its social attractiveness and power made teaching potentially dangerous. The desire to be in the spotlight as the spokesperson and authority was a problem then as it is now. We must help immature and undisciplined speakers grow before we give them platforms. We must help new Christians grow in knowledge and make sure they possess in their personal experience what they profess with their words before we give them positions of influence and up-front public speaking opportunities.

TEACHERS' MISTAKES
In New Testament times, many teachers failed and misused their positions of responsibility. Some of the teachers:
- Introduced Judaism, Mosaic laws, and circumcision (Acts 15:24), weakening the gospel truth that we are saved by grace alone
- Lived in contradiction to what they taught (Romans 2:17-29)
- Taught before they knew anything themselves (1 Timothy 1:6-7)
- Catered to people's "itching ears" (2 Timothy 4:3)

WHAT ARE MY MOTIVES FOR BEING A TEACHER?

Those who take on teaching roles should ask themselves the following questions as a way of evaluating their fitness to teach:

- Am I teaching as an act of service?
- Am I trying to advance my own status or position in the church?
- Am I teaching to discharge a duty?

Christian teachers need to be primarily models of integrity and secondarily instructors of content; therefore, they should submit both their lives and their words to God's scrutiny. Their teaching must not be frivolous or selfish. Teachers should teach God's truth, not merely their own opinions. If we teach others, we must make sure that our lives do not contradict what we teach.

3:2 **We all stumble in many ways.** NIV We all make mistakes or slip up when we are off guard. We all stumble, but our most frequent failures occur when we are speaking. To "stumble" means to go astray or sin. The fact that we all sin in many ways is illustrated frequently in the Bible (see 2 Chronicles 6:36; Psalm 19:13; Proverbs 20:9; Romans 7:14-16; 1 John 1:8, 10). Because we are prone to make mistakes in our speech, we need to be even more careful to let God control what we say. He is capable of guiding our motivation, our thoughts, our very choice of words, and even the impact our communication has on others.

The ease with which we all stumble is James's second reason for cautioning those who want to teach. The first was the weight of greater responsibility. Teachers are not just people who are mature enough not to stumble—they also ought to be those who correctly handle their failures. Believers are frequently guilty of putting immature Christians (for example, newly converted celebrities) into positions of authority and then being disappointed when these young believers are not able to live up to the expectations placed on them.

If anyone is never at fault in what he says, he is a perfect man. NIV *Perfect* here means mature or complete. Many people may think that it is impossible to control the tongue, but most people haven't even begun to try. The ability to control the tongue is the mark of true maturity for the Christian (see 1:19, "be slow to speak"). When Jesus confronted the religious leaders about their accusations against him, he said that out of the abundance of the heart the mouth speaks—showing that what is inside of a person affects what they do with their speech (Matthew 12:33-37). He also said that we must give account for every careless word we utter (Matthew 12:36). (See Proverbs 15:1-4 for more on how a mature person controls his or her tongue.)

Able to keep the whole body in check. NRSV The expression *in check* (*chalinagogesai*) means "to bridle," which introduces the analogies James uses next. James is saying that anyone who can control his or her mouth will be able to control the rest of his or her body. The wisdom and love from God and the self-restraint given by the Holy Spirit will help us exercise this control.

One of the greatest forms friendship can take is the willingness of one friend to correct with compassion the speaking of the other. When someone points out something wrong we said, or a hurtful way of speaking, our first response may be defensive. But we must learn that a true friend cares for us, including the way we talk. Are we willing to genuinely care for that person in the same way?

3:3-5 Bits . . . rudder . . . tongue. What do these things have in common? They are all small but very effective controllers—they each direct something much larger than themselves. James is building a case for the damaging power of our words. We see this evidenced in history when dictators such as Adolph Hitler, the Ayatollah Khomeini, Joseph Stalin, and Saddam Hussein used their words to mobilize people to destroy others. We see it evidenced in church splits and in the running of a pastor's reputation. And we see how verbal abuse in the home can destroy the very personhood and character of spouses and children.

3:3 Bits . . . make them obey us. NIV If a person's impulsive speech is uncontrolled, his or her whole life is headed in the wrong direction. Horses are larger and stronger than people, but they can be turned with a small bit in the mouth. We should let Christ bridle our mouths instead of speaking out every time a thoughtless word comes to mind. From this point on, James shows that not only teaching, but all forms of speech can be powerfully beneficial or destructive.

3:4 Ships . . . are so large. Ships were some of the largest and most powerful man-made structures known by early Christians. Ships moved tons of cargo across the sea. Reminding his readers that a large and powerful oceangoing vessel could be controlled by a small rudder, James drives home the point of how powerful and pivotal the tongue can be. In our time we have seen how oil spills from large tankers can cause billions of dollars of damage, all because of an uncontrolled rudder. Small things control much. The use of the tongue has split churches and destroyed lives. We can use our speech in impulsive, automatic, and thoughtless ways, lashing out at others and passing on gossip. Without control, destruction is sure to follow.

ARE YOU UNDER CONTROL?

What we say and what we *don't* say are both important. Proper speech is not only saying the right words at the right time, it is also controlling our desire to say what we shouldn't.

Examples of an untamed tongue include: gossiping, belittling, cursing, bragging, manipulating, false teaching, exaggerating, complaining, flattering, and lying. Before speaking we should ask, "Is this what I really want to say? Is it true? Is it necessary? Is it kind?"

In Colossians 3:5-11, Paul associates eliminating sins of speech with the stripping off of the old self. This can only be accomplished by God working in us.

3:5 **The tongue is a small part of the body.**[NIV] As the bit, the rudder, and the spark, the tongue is a small but influential part of the body. Since the mouth reflects and directs our lifestyle, we must learn to control it. Anything capable of such great evil must also be capable of great good. Paul taught that the whole body, including the tongue, ought to be considered a "living sacrifice" (Romans 12:1) to God.

A great forest is set on fire by a small spark.[NIV] During the dry season in Israel, the grass, low thornbushes, and scrubs were as dry as explosive tinder. One spark could spread a wild fire. The first two analogies (bit and rudder) were directed at the tongue's effect on the person. The spark analogy speaks to the effect of the tongue beyond the person. This illustrates the following warnings:

- *Our words have wide-ranging impact.* They are able to kill at a distance. Not only do they hurt people face-to-face, but like long-range missiles they can be launched from a remote conversation, or like mine fields they can be planted to do their damage much later. Innuendo may be regarded as fact. Juicy tidbits may be repeated and cause their damage long after they are started.

- *We can't control the effects of our words.* In tinder dry conditions, a forest fire can quickly burn out of control. Likewise, a rumor can take off and take on a life of its own. We must carefully monitor what we say.

Satan uses the tongue to divide people and pit them against one another. Idle words are damaging because they quickly spread destruction. We dare not be careless with our words, thinking that we can apologize later, because even when we do, the damage remains. A few words spoken in anger can destroy a relationship that took years to build. Remember that words are like fire; they can neither control nor reverse the damage they do. For example, a public figure's reputation can be greatly harmed by a quote taken out of context or a false allegation.

> A sharp tongue is the only edged tool that grows keener with constant use.
> *Washington Irving*

3:6 **A world of evil.** NIV The tongue is the source of all kinds of evil because of the damage it can cause in the world and bring to the rest of the Christian community.

WORD PICTURES ON THE IMPORTANCE OF OUR SPEECH

In James 3, several word pictures are used to show the importance of mature speech.

BIT	A small bit controls a large animal.	Can we control our use of the tongue?
RUDDER	A small piece of wood steers a huge ship in heavy wind.	The tongue, though small, can create grave consequences.
FIRE	A small spark unleashes a destructive force.	Do we recognize the destructive force our words can have?
ANIMALS	People can tame animals.	Can we tame our speech and our impulsive thoughts?
POISON	The venom of a snake kills its prey.	Can we keep our words from poisoning us and others?
SPRING	A spring can produce only one kind of water.	Is our speech a spring that's good or foul?
FIG TREE	Trees bear just one kind of fruit.	Is our speech bearing good fruit, or is it mixed with bad?
TONGUE	The tongue can be used for good or evil.	Does our speech reflect our Christian maturity?

Sets the course of nature. NKJV The uncontrolled tongue can set our entire human existence on fire. The NRSV translates "the course of nature" as "the cycle of nature" (literally, "the wheel of being"). The expression was used in ancient times to indicate "the ups and downs in life," as well as one's entire human existence.

This means that the tongue can destroy all the good that we've built up over a lifetime. While we have ministered for years and years and seen abundant fruit, if we fail to control the tongue, we can undo all the good we have built up in our years of ministry. Our speech has a power that few other capabilities possess.

> This slender portion
> of flesh contains the
> whole world of iniquity.
>
> *John Calvin*

Set on fire by hell. The verb implies habitual action. In other words, the tongue keeps on setting on fire and inflaming our passions. It inflames our temper; it leads us to actions that are displeasing to God. Even intelligent people can behave like fools when reacting to unthoughtful criticism. They become inflamed by the use of the tongue.

Flames of hate, prejudice, slander, jealousy, and envy seem to come from the very lake of fire where Satan will be punished (see Revelation 20:10, 14-15 for more on the lake of fire).

WHAT IS HELL?

"Hell" in Greek is *gehenna*. Gehenna was named after the Valley of Hinnom, a spot just south of Jerusalem where the garbage was burned, and where human sacrifice had been made (2 Kings 21:1-18). Constant fire represents eternal punishment; thus Gehenna is the same as "the lake of fire" (Revelation 20:10, 14-15). Gehenna is not the same as Hades, which is the place where both good and bad went after death. Gehenna is also mentioned in Matthew 5:22.

3:7 All kinds of animals . . . have been tamed by man. NIV Genesis 1:28 states: "God blessed them and said to them, 'Be fruitful and increase in number; fill the earth and subdue it. Rule over the fish of the sea and the birds of the air and over every living creature that moves on the ground'" (NIV). Genesis 9:2 says: "The fear and dread of you will fall upon all the beasts of the earth and all the birds of the air, upon every creature that moves along the ground, and upon all the fish of the sea; they are given into your hands" (NIV). Psalm 8:6-8 also echoes the fact that God has given dominion to humanity over all the animals. Human ingenuity has tamed wild creatures to make them useful. But no person, by his own unaided power, can restrain the tongue.

3:8 **No one can tame the tongue.** NRSV Proverbs 13:3 says, "He who guards his lips guards his life." So what hope is there for taming the tongue? We are helpless . . . unless we get help.

No person can tame the tongue, but Christ can. To do it, he goes straight for the heart (Mark 7:14-15; Psalm 51:10) and the mind (Romans 12:1-2). We should not try to control our tongue with our own strength; we should rely on the Holy Spirit. He will give us increasing power to monitor and control what we say. For when we feel offended or unjustly criticized, the Spirit will remind us of God's love and keep us from reacting. The Holy Spirit will heal the hurt and keep us from lashing out. We can make sure we are in the Spirit's control by incorporating Scripture into our life and by asking the Spirit to direct our thoughts and actions each day.

> He does not say no one
> can tame the tongue,
> but no one of men: so
> that when it is tamed
> we confess that this is
> brought about by the
> pity, the help, and the
> grace of God.
>
> *Augustine*

A restless evil. NRSV *Restless* means unstable and incapable of restraint. The tongue is always capable of evil; it remains untamed throughout life. With our tongue we can lash out and destroy. By recognizing the tongue's deadly capacity, we can take the first steps to keep it under control.

Full of deadly poison. What we say can be dangerous and deadly, carrying poison that drips long after the words are spoken. David said in Psalm 140:3, "They make their tongues as sharp as a serpent's; the poison of vipers is on their lips."

EXCUSES FOR SPEAKING YOUR MIND
Contemporary wisdom says that people should assert themselves and say what they really feel; speak out, rather than stifle. There are many rationalizations for the unrestrained use of the tongue. We say:

- "Somebody had to tell him off."
- "It was good to get it off my chest."
- "I sure gave her a piece of my mind."
- "Maybe what I said will do him some good."
- "I felt better for saying it."

Instead of making excuses for sounding off, we can exercise restraint and allow God's peace and wisdom to guide what we say.

Our society encourages us to speak out in a thoughtless way, totally disregarding the deadly impact our words may have. Christ's attitude is for us to deal with our anger and frustration honestly and maturely but to use restraint in how we reveal these feelings to others.

3:9 **With the tongue we praise our Lord and Father.**NIV Praising God or blessing was a normal daily practice for Jews and Jewish Christians, thus using the tongue to curse others should have seemed abnormal. The blessing of God was a common practice in Jewish devotional life. "The Holy One, Blessed is He" is one of the most frequent descriptions of God in rabbinic literature. The "Eighteen Benedictions," a liturgical formula used daily by righteous Jews, concluded each of its parts with the blessing of God. *Lord and Father* is used only here in the New Testament. Paul's favorite reference to God was "the God and Father of our Lord Jesus Christ" (Romans 15:6; 2 Corinthians 1:3; Ephesians 1:3).

We curse those who are made in the likeness of God.NRSV We should have the same attitude of respect for fellow human beings as we have for God, because they are created in his image. Yet we have this horrible, double-sided tongue.

TWO USES OF THE TONGUE

In *The Pilgrim's Progress*, John Bunyan describes the character Talkative as "a saint abroad and a devil at home." Sometimes we show great courtesy to strangers, but then are impatient and irritable with our families. We may be compliant at work but then be verbally abusive to our spouse or children. We may gladly repeat spiritual insights on Sunday but then pass on suggestive stories during the week. We may be sweet and gracious at a Bible study, but then immediately afterwards destroy someone's reputation with our gossip. We may praise our Lord and curse people. How easily we tolerate slander and backbiting. We benefit from worship yet we may excuse destructive talk and gossiping. And we may hesistate to correct others who gossip, tear others down, or criticize destructively.

Some people think that the only restraint against foul talk, calling people names, and bad language is social disapproval. But God's Word condemns it. James says that the reason we should not curse people is because they have been made in God's likeness. We should not use any word or name that reduces them to anything less than their full stature as God's created beings. The doctrine of "total depravity" doesn't mean that the image of God is obliterated in a person, but only that every aspect of our being is affected by sin. There is still something in the sinner worth saving. That is why Christ came to die.

3:10 Out of the same mouth come praise and cursing. [NIV] James knew that followers of Christ might be capable of both praise and cursing because of what he had observed in the disciples. Peter promised Christ, "I will not deny you" (Matthew 26:35 NRSV), but then he denied Jesus with oaths and curses (Matthew 26:69-75). In 1 John 3:18, the apostle John says, "Dear children, let us not love with words or tongue but with actions and in truth" (NIV). Earlier in his life, John was willing to call down fire to destroy a Samaritan village (Luke 9:51-56). Because speech reveals a person's heart, it exhibits the same potential to help or destroy. The tongue reflects the inner person (Matthew 12:34).

The deceitful, dual use of the tongue is the result of double-mindedness, fickleness, and the instability of a life that is ruled by impulse rather than by the love of God. The tongue reveals either maturity or immaturity. It gives a picture of our basic human nature, made in God's image but fallen into sin. God works to change us from the inside out. As the Holy Spirit purifies our heart, he gives us self-control so that we will speak words that please God. Instead of fighting, we need to be helpful, positive, and encouraging toward others.

3:11 Can both fresh water and salt water flow from the same spring? [NIV] James pictures the inner being, the heart, as a spring. Jesus used the same illustration in his conversation with the Samaritan woman: "But whoever drinks the water I give him will never thirst. Indeed, the water I give him will become in him a spring of water welling up to eternal life" (John 4:14 NIV). There were many springs and wells throughout the ancient land of Israel.

WHAT SPRINGS FROM YOU?
Many of James's readers knew that some springs had been contaminated by salty water, and some had gone brackish and foul. But others still bubbled up safe and clean water. It would be like comparing the fresh-flowing Jordan River with the salty Dead Sea. Although different kinds of water won't bubble from the same opening, Christians' speech can be very inconsistent. One time we may speak in a way that honors God and another time in a way that gives Satan power to operate. We can choose how we will respond. If we do not, we give Satan an opening to control us.

3:12 Can a fig tree . . . yield olives? [NRSV] Jesus used the same illustration in Matthew 7:16-20; 12:33-35; and Luke 6:43-45. We should produce the kind of fruit that we've been created and regenerated to produce—the fruit of righteousness (see James 3:18).

No spring yields both salt water and fresh. NKJV The implication from this answer to the question in 3:11 is that only a renewed heart can produce pure speech. Only Christ can change us as God changed the bitter water for the people of Israel at Marah (Exodus 15:23-25). This event is used repeatedly in Scripture as an illustration of the danger of complaining.

If the source of our thoughts and actions is the love of God in our life, then we will not be able to generate the kind of negative speech that James warns us against.

> If a cup is filled only with good water, it cannot spill even one drop of bitter water, no matter how badly it is jarred.
>
> *Oswald Chambers*

BRINGING OUR SPEECH UNDER GOD'S CONTROL

To help bring our speech under God's control we can:

- Count our blessings. By focusing on the positive, we will take away the anger and bitterness from our spirit that leads us to make negative comments or accusations towards others.
- Get in touch with the love of God. As we allow God to satisfy our spiritual needs, we will have less of a need to strike out at others.
- Write our thoughts in a letter instead of lashing out. We can pour out our inner feelings, and then not send the letter. Instead, we should pray over the letter and ask God to give us a change of attitude and spirit.
- Wait before responding to a comment, criticism, or piece of gossip.
- Make five positive comments to every negative one that we make about someone else.
- Treat everything we say as a gift to another person. We should ask: "Are my words a gift that I truly want to leave in their hands?"

WISDOM FROM HEAVEN / 3:13-18

James lays down a challenge before the church for those who claim to have true wisdom: they need to observe the true wisdom that comes from heaven. The church James wrote to was a church under pressure. When under pressure, a church can split into factions. There was no formal clergy or ordination process, so self-styled teachers could emerge, claiming to have wisdom. As each teacher promoted his brand of wisdom and gained a following, the community of believers was divided. In the New Testament church there were many problems with factions or a "party spirit" (see Acts 6; 1 Corinthians 1; see also Philippians 1:17; 2:3).

Jesus taught that we would know true teachers from false ones by how they lived (Matthew 7:15-23). Good teachers will exemplify good life disciplines. Their activities, actions, and accomplishments will reveal the true heart of their Christian faith. In this section, good deeds are contrasted with bitterness, and humility is contrasted with selfish ambition.

3:13 Who is wise and understanding? This is a rhetorical question answered by James in the next phrase. The truly wise person demonstrates his or her understanding of Christ by the way he or she lives. Few people are foolish enough to openly claim to be wise. But most do want to live effective lives. We would like our words and thoughts to be significant to others. And yet wisdom is not a characteristic we can claim for ourselves. It is a quality recognized by others. True wisdom is measured by the depth of a person's character.

Joseph's life (see Genesis 37–50) is a shining example of wise living. His experience certainly had its share of trials and temptations: sold into slavery by his brothers, sexually harassed, unjustly imprisoned. Joseph could have despaired many times. Yet he trusted God. He did not know what the future held, but he did know who held his future. He concentrated on what the events of his life required of him rather than being overly concerned with what others were doing. Joseph's trust was vindicated. We can expect God to respond to our trust in the same way.

Let him show it by his good life. [NIV] Our works show where our hearts are invested (Matthew 6:19-21, 33). Do our attitudes and motives match our actions? While we may not claim to be wise, we can aim at living in wise ways. The guidance given to us in God's Word is dependable wisdom. The specific qualities James is about to list ought to be part of our ongoing prayers, and they ought to be part of the intentions of our life.

Humility that comes from wisdom. [NIV] False humility is ruled out. We are not to be hypocrites who pretend to be humble, using "humility" to impress others. Instead, we should take an accurate look at ourselves. "Be honest in your estimate of yourselves" (Romans 12:3 [TLB]). And we should watch out for pride in our relationships with others. Pride is having an attitude of self-importance about the talents and abilities that God has given us and using them to set ourselves up as superior or to be divisive in our relationships with others.

Wisdom, then, involves both actions and attitudes in living. A wise life will display not only goodness, but also humility.

3:14 **Bitter envy and selfish ambition.** NRSV What is the relationship of worldly wisdom to ambition? Why is ambition so harmful? Our selfish nature can **harbor** and become saturated with bitter envy and selfish ambition. Bitter envy is misguided zeal that results in contentiousness. It is anger at the accomplishments of others. Whenever we find fault with a leader, we must ask ourselves what is motivating us to feel strongly about that person's failure. Do we actually share the same weakness? Do we imagine ourselves doing better in that role? Or are we in fact, simply envious of the abilities or success God has allowed him or her to have? A positive answer to any of these ought to make us very careful in how we express our criticisms.

Here and in Philippians 2:3, *selfish ambition* refers to leaders in the church who are developing a "party spirit." This party spirit is produced when our ambition leads us to split the church in order to develop a certain "party" mentality among others, who blindly follow. This produces factions who are for or against the pastor or certain programs, who take sides on issues not necessarily central to the Christian faith.

Selfish ambition is the desire to live for one's self and no one or nothing else, only for what we can get out of it. In our desperate attempts to persuade others to see our point of view, we may lose our sense of reason and conviction and become fanatical. Then we will want to wipe out those who persistently oppose or disagree with us. This leads to bitterness. We want to win. We want to be right—to have the last word at all costs. This is what it means to be selfishly ambitious. Having confidence in only our knowledge, we arrogantly lord it over others. (See 1 Peter 5:3 for more on being concerned for what we can give rather than what we can get.)

Do not boast. NKJV When our true motives are exposed, one defense is to become arrogant. Our very pride ought to tell us that our desire to be seen as wise is based on selfishness. The moment that we least want to admit our pride is the moment when recognizing it will do us the most good.

Deny the truth. NIV The specific truth to which James is referring is the truth that we might be harboring bitter envy and selfish ambition. But resisting truth in one way can easily lead to resisting truth in general. Denying the truth or speaking against the truth is a chief characteristic of the devil mentioned in John 8:44, where he is called the "father of lies." To talk as if we are wise and good when our life denies it is the lie for which Paul condemned the Jewish Christians (Romans 2:17, 23).

3:15 Such wisdom . . . is earthly. The source and standards of this kind of wisdom are from the world and not God. Its teachers are self-centered and shallow.

This wisdom doesn't come from faith—it is godless and **unspiritual.** *Unspiritual* (NRSV) could refer to the natural man. The term for unspiritual is used in the New Testament for the person who does not have God's Spirit (3:15), or does not accept the guidance that comes from the Spirit of God (1 Corinthians 2:14). This person teaches only the wisdom of this life. His or her wisdom is based on human feelings and human reasoning alone without God's help.

Of the devil.NIV The real source of these thoughts is the devil. It is foolhardy for believers to assume that Satan does not have access to most of the knowledge available to us. From the devil's point of view, the temptation of Jesus (Matthew 4) was a wise plan, wisely carried out. Satan even used Scripture in making his suggestions to Jesus seem reasonable. He failed because he was up against real wisdom. The devil still makes use of the same resources that God has provided for us. But his purposes are destructive; they can produce a climate in the church, at home, and at work that damages relationships. Think of how quickly our words, language, and tone of voice can create a destructive climate.

3:16-17 Disorder and wickedness of every kind.NRSV Jealous people think they must be first in everything. They cannot stand to see anyone else in the limelight, or have anyone else cast a shadow on what they do. This leads to desires and strategies for revenge that can lead to chaos.

The wisdom from above.NRSV The following seven characteristics of heavenly wisdom are strung together like pearls. They are what wisdom does. These qualities are seen in Christ's character and are also embodied in the famous chapter on love (1 Corinthians 13). Do you desire these qualities for your life? Have you prayed for God's help to exemplify them in your life?

First indicates that this is a main characteristic and a key to the others, not just number one.

Pure. We must be pure enough to approach God. To be fruitful for him, we must have moral and spiritual integrity.

Peaceable.NKJV This is peace that goes beyond inner peace; it is opposed to strife. It is peace between people, and between people and God. It must be peace that affects the community. Christians must not only prefer peace, but they should also seek to spread it. Since chapters 3 and 4 deal with dissension, purity must be understood as a key trait of a peacemaker—one who can withstand those who attempt to split the church.

Considerate.NIV This is the opposite of self-seeking. It does not demand its own right. It goes beyond the strict requirements of justice. To be kindly and considerate is to make allowances for others, to temper justice with mercy. It is the kind of treatment that we would like to receive from others.

Willing to yield.NRSV Heavenly wisdom is reasonable, flexible—willing to listen and to change. Just as good soldiers willingly follow orders from their superiors, people with heavenly wisdom willingly follow God's orders and respond to his correction.

Full of mercy and good fruits.NKJV God's wisdom is full of God's gracious forgiveness. And his love leads to practical action, helping and serving others. We should be willing to forgive even when the problems we are facing are someone else's fault.

ImpartialNIV means to be single-minded and free from prejudice toward people and without double-mindedness toward God (1:5-8).

TWO TYPES OF WISDOM

WISDOM FROM BELOW

Characterized by:
Bitter envy (v. 14)
Selfish ambition (v. 14)
Boasting (v. 14)
Denying the truth (v. 14)
Being earthly-minded (v. 15)
Being unspiritual (v. 15)
From the devil (v. 15)

Resulting in:
Disorder (v. 16)
Evil practices/actions (v. 16)

WISDOM FROM HEAVEN

Characterized by:
Purity (v. 17)—personal transparency or holiness
Peaceable (v. 17)—willing to sacrifice for peace
Considerate (v. 17)—gentle, not seeking its own way
Willing to yield (v. 17)—agreeable, willing to reevaluate, open
Merciful (v. 17)—compassionate
Impartial (v. 17)—single-minded toward God and people
Sincere (v. 17)—without hypocrisy

Resulting in:
Good fruit (v. 17)
Righteousness/good actions (v. 18)

Sincere.[NIV] According to the Greek (*anupokritos*), this word means "unhypocritical." God's wisdom makes people genuine.

3:18 Peacemakers who sow in peace raise a harvest of righteousness.[NIV] William Barclay paraphrases this as follows: "For the seed that one day produces the reward that righteousness brings can only be sown when personal relationships are right and by those whose contacts produce such relationships." (For more on sowing wisdom and truth and reaping righteousness see Psalm 1:3; Proverbs 11:30; Galatians 6:7-10; Philippians 1:11.)

This section gives three suggestions for controlling the tongue:

1. Seek God's wisdom.

2. Admit jealousy and arrogance without trying to cover them up.

3. Create a climate of peace wherever God leads you.

In Matthew 5:9, Jesus promises that the peacemakers will be blessed. Their reward will be to see right relationships between God and people.

James 4

SUBMIT YOURSELVES TO GOD / 4:1-12

At the end of chapter 3, James explains that false wisdom leads to disorder and every evil practice (3:16), and that true wisdom results in good fruit (3:17) and righteousness (3:18). From this poetic description of wisdom expressed in general terms, James returns to practical application. His readers need to know what wisdom is, but they need even more to live wisely. Chapter 4 begins with a challenge to behavior that James saw as proof of demonic wisdom—fights and quarrels among them. His questions take on the firmness and commitment of a person who understands that unchallenged evil will not go away. James wants his brothers and sisters to resist not only the practices of evil wisdom, but also the source from which this wisdom springs. His plan requires a declaration of allegiance to God and open rebellion from the devil's ranks.

We need to feel the impact of these same truths as James describes situations that are only too true in churches today. The fights and quarrels that James observed still characterize the life of the body of Christ and seriously hamper the effective communication of the gospel. Outsiders who look to the church as a place of solace and salvation often find it is full of strife and danger. We desperately need God's wisdom in our churches.

4:1 Those conflicts and disputes among you, where do they come from?NRSV The first term (*polemoi*) refers to a battle with weapons, an armed conflict. It was used figuratively to indicate the struggle between powers, both earthly and spiritual. This is followed by *machai*, which refers to fighting, but without weapons, as in personal conflicts. James is describing a condition where a group has come to a state of war, with open skirmishes breaking out among people. Sides have been chosen, positions have been dug in, and anyone seeking to be neutral is looked on with suspicion by both sides. In cases like this, believers have ceased being peacemakers who sow in peace (3:18). Instead, they live in open antagonism toward one another. These conflicts have nothing to do with quarrels with the pagan world; these are quarrels within the church, among believers.

We cannot brush aside James's question. He doesn't waste time saying that these conflicts should not occur. When they do happen, are we wise enough to understand why? Do we know their source? Fortunately, most of us have experienced the conflicts that James describes as temporary struggles in local churches. When handled correctly, with godly wisdom, they can lead to growth. Sadly, however, some churches become permanent battlegrounds. New believers find themselves in a cross fire of arguments, resentments, and power struggles that may carry a veneer of spiritual truth, but are more often simply personal conflicts between people. In the process, innocent bystanders are sometimes deeply wounded. Many of us know people who have been alienated from the church because of a conflict that had nothing to do with the gospel. These battles and the issues at stake remind us of Jesus' words concerning people with twisted religious priorities: "But if anyone causes one of these little ones who believe in me to sin, it would be better for him to have a large millstone

I have often wondered that persons who make boast of professing the Christian religion —namely love, joy, peace, temperance, and charity to all men— should quarrel with such rancorous animosity, and display daily towards one another such bitter hatred, that this, rather than the virtues which they profess, is the readiest criteria of their faith. *Benedict Spinoza*

THE DOWNWARD SPIRAL OF OUR DESIRES

Without submission to God, our desires lead us down a well-worn path that will harm us and those around us (see James 1:14-15; 4:1-3).

Unchecked desires ——————— lead to

Not asking God ——————— lead to

Coveting, evil desires, wrong motives ——————— leads to

Fights and quarrels ——————— lead to

Church life marked by death (slander, judging others, name calling, boasting, backbiting) ——————— lead to hung around his neck and to be drowned in the depths of the sea" (Matthew 18:1-9; Luke 11:37-54).

Fights and quarrels are being caused, not by some external source, but by the people's cravings or "pleasures." James is convinced the truth is plain to see. He asks a question, and he expects us to agree. The Greek word for pleasure, *hedone*, is the source of the English word *hedonism*, the philosophy that pleasure is the main goal of life. When everyone seeks his or her own pleasure, only strife, hatred, and division can result. James has already warned us that our desires (*epithumia*) in general are the means of temptation (1:14-15). The desires of which he is speaking here are more specific. They are a "desire" (NIV), or a pleasure-motivated need, battling to be satisfied. James uses military imagery to show that we are in a very real struggle. The battle within is expressed by the word *strateuomenon* (warring), a word suggesting a raging battle, fought between the desire to do good and the desire to do evil. Paul gives a personal testimony of this internal warfare in Romans 7:7-25.

When we lose the battle and so fulfill our internal evil desires, we create conflicts on the outside. People who are battling to fulfill their own desires eventually begin to compete for the limited amounts of power, prestige, or possessions that promise to bring pleasure. People are suddenly competitors, no longer friends or Christian brothers and sisters. The fierce competition drives people to shameful thoughts and actions, and quickly makes them unable to pray correctly.

Desire for the pleasures of the world always threatens our spiritual life (see Luke 8:14; Titus 3:3). Because believers are unable to divide their loyalty between God and the world (4:4), there will continue to be this battle within them.

> Is it not because of this passion that relations are broken, and this natural goodwill changed into desperate enmity? that great and populous countries are desolated by domestic dissensions? and land and sea filled with ever new disasters by naval battles and land campaigns? For the wars famous in tragedy . . . have all flowed from one source— desire either for money or glory or pleasure. Over these things the human race goes mad.
>
> *Philo*, on why "desire" (covetousness) is forbidden in the Ten Commandments

4:2 You want something and do not have it. NRSV A frustrated desire is a bomb that must be defused. If not, when it explodes it will not obtain what it wanted and may destroy everything nearby.

This is the result of an attitude that says, "If I can't have what I want, no one else will have it either!"

CHURCH WARS

Weapons and strategies are used in church fights and quarrels.

Missiles	Attacking church members from long range.
Guerrilla tactics	Ambushing the unsuspecting.
Snipers	Well-aimed criticism.
Terrorism	No one is immune from being hurt.
Mines	Ensuring that others will fail in their efforts to serve God.
Espionage	Using friendships to get potentially damaging information about others.
Propaganda	Using gossip to spread damaging information about others.
Cold war	Freezing out an opponent by withdrawing or refusing to talk to him or her.
Nuclear attack	Being willing to sacrifice the church if the goals of my group are not met.

James tells us the exact location of the manufacturing plants for all these weapons. The trouble is in ourselves.

The craving described here becomes so strong that the people "kill and covet" (NIV) to obtain what they want. Are people actually guilty of murdering others when they fulfill their desires? James's expression begs a thoughtful answer. People are, in fact, capable of killing in pursuit of desires or as a reaction to frustrated desires. Our shock over the leap from "wanting" to "murdering" must be tempered by remembering how Jesus took the key words of the Ten Commandments and gave them applications that strike very close to home. For Jesus, the commandment against murdering applied equally to verbal assassination as to physical killing (see Matthew 5:21-22; see also 1 John 3:15). The word *kill* can be taken as a hyperbole for bitter hatred. But desires, if not controlled, could lead to such extreme violence. Hardly a week goes by without some story in the news of a person who, claiming to love another deeply, ends up murdering that person because the "love" was not returned in kind.

Instead of rethinking their desires, the people being described by James resort to evil, verbal abuse, jealousy, and worse. Yet, for all their anxious self-seeking and antagonism in getting what they want, they still don't get it. Why?

You do not have, because you do not ask God.[NIV] The first readers of this letter were lusting, scheming, and fighting instead of praying. They were lacking at several levels:

- By ignoring God, they demonstrated a lack of regard for his presence and power to help them.

- They lacked godly wisdom because they refused to "ask God, who gives generously to all without finding fault, and it will be given to him" (1:5).

- They lacked what they really needed because they did not rely on God. Instead, they depended on their desires to guide them.

We learned (from getting our first tricycle or doll to driving our first new car) that fulfilled desires don't satisfy at the level they advertise. Sometimes we actually do get just what we *wanted*, only to discover that we still do not have what we really *needed*—the deep contentment that only comes when we are right with God. Trusted alone, our desires will only lead us to the things of this earth and not to the things of God.

In summary, James's message is: "You don't have what you desire because you don't desire God." James is preparing us for a crucial lesson: Until we look at all of life, including our strongest desires, from the perspective of God's plans and priorities for us, our life will be constantly hounded by the awareness that we do not have.

WHEN IS IT TIME TO PRAY?
James mentions the most common problems in prayer: not asking, asking for the wrong things, asking for the wrong reasons. Do we talk to God at all? When we do, what do we talk about? Do we ask only to satisfy our desires? Do we seek God's approval for what we already plan to do? Our prayers will become powerful when we allow God to change our desires so that they perfectly correspond to his will for us (1 John 3:21-22).

4:3   You ask. Almost as bad as not asking is asking wrongly. If we misunderstand the correct use of prayer, we might not pray at all, or we might attempt to manipulate God. Later, James makes it clear that, when we pray, we must submit to God (4:7). Otherwise we will not be answered.

You do not receive, because you ask with wrong motives. NIV People should not be surprised when their prayers go unanswered because they often ask with wrong motives. They were going to **spend** what they received on their **pleasures** (the same word as "desires" in 4:1 NIV). Their "spending" would be like that of the prodigal son who squandered his inheritance on himself (Luke 15:14). The people's desires were so strong that they were fighting, quarreling, and then using prayer to get what they wanted. Their motives were not to help others, but to satisfy themselves.

> This is not the trusting child asking for a meal, but the greedy child asking for the best piece or the spoiled child demanding his or her own way.
>
> *Peter H. Davids*

THINK BEFORE YOU PRAY
Unexamined prayers degenerate into clichés and wish lists. James confronted the tendency to pray carelessly. Could our prayers be open to being corrupted or contaminated by bad motives? We are repelled by the sight of a beautiful stream spoiled by toxic waste, or by industrial smoke fouling the air. But we may barely notice when selfish desires contaminate our prayers. While it is true that God gives us permission to ask for anything (see John 14:13-14; Philippians 4:6), we need to reexamine our requests from time to time, especially those that God does not grant. Several questions can help us in this process:

- Do I really need what I have asked for?
- Am I asking for special treatment from God?
- Is it in the best interest of God's kingdom and his will that I receive this request?
- What do I plan to do when God grants my request?

Prayers are not automatically answered with a yes from God. Although God gives many promises about the power of prayer (see Matthew 7:7-11; 17:20; Mark 11:23-24; Luke 18:1-8; John 14:13-14), these promises hinge upon the attitude of the person praying—how in tune he or she is with God. True prayer must express dependence on God. Especially when we are praying for ourselves, our attitude must be "Your will be done." A selfish person cannot say that to God.

4:4 Adulterers. NRSV The shocking word *adulterers* (literally "adulteresses!") graphically describes the spiritual unfaithfulness of the people and intends to jar them into facing their true spiritual condition. The concept of adultery against God is taken from the

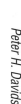

Old Testament (see Isaiah 54:5; Jeremiah 3:20; Ezekiel 16:15-19; Hosea 2:2-5; 3:1-5; 9:1). When God's people, Israel, turned to idolatry, they tried to combine the worship of God and the worship of Baal. Like an adulterous wife, they wanted the husband and home, but also wanted the lover. James is about to describe these believers as adulterous because they are trying to love God *and* have an affair with the world.

The struggle of James's original readers is not unique to their lives. The fact that God would express in the strongest terms possible the importance of faithfulness ought to unsettle us. Biblical standards of personal, marital, and spiritual behavior are under a constant attack of erosion. We are bombarded with the message to compromise.

From the world's point of view, we should be flexible, tolerant of sin, and accommodating. But it won't work, because **friend-ship with the world is enmity with God.**NKJV For believers,

NO MIDDLE GROUND
Why is it impossible to be a friend of the world and a friend of God at the same time? The paths lead in opposite directions and to very different conclusions:

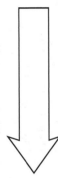

Faith, Hope, Love (1 Corinthians 13:13)
Love, Joy, Peace . . . (Galatians 5:22)
Abundant Living (John 10:10)
Eternal Life (John 3:16)
Love of Neighbor (Matthew 7:12)

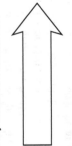

Strife/Quarrels (James 4:1-3)
Materialism (1 John 2:15-17)
Hopelessness (Ephesians 2:12)
Egocentric Living (James 4:3)
Death (Proverbs 14:12)

the world and God are two distinct objects of affection, but they are direct opposites. What then is friendship with the world? The word for *world* (*kosmos*) refers to the system of evil under Satan's control, all that is opposed to God. To be friendly with the world, then, is to adopt its values and desires (see also Romans 8:7-8; 2 Timothy 4:10; 1 John 2:15-17). The believers may indeed love God, but they are also infatuated with the benefits of this world's system. They worship God, but they want the influence, living standards, financial security, and perhaps some of the freedom the world offers. These pursuits will only undermine the generosity, caring, and sharing that should characterize Christians.

IS PLEASURE WRONG?
Many people worry that the warning against "friendship with the world" prohibits seeking influence, security, and a better standard of living. Such pursuits may not be wrong in themselves, but it is pursuing these things without reference to God or his ways that is wrong. It is disregarding God's rightful claim on all our time and resources, acting as if they were our own creation and possession. It is using people and things for our own goals and desires and not seeking to serve and obey him in all our relationships and dealings. None of our pursuits in life should violate our ultimate allegiance to God and required obedience to him.

Nothing is wrong with wanting a pleasurable life. God gives us good gifts to enjoy (1:17; Ephesians 4:7; 1 Timothy 4:4-5). But having friendship with the world involves seeking pleasure at others' expense or by disobeying God. Pleasure that keeps us from pleasing God is sinful; pleasure that comes from God's rich bounty is good.

If we are forbidden as believers to have a friendship with the world, what then is our proper relationship to the world? Some have used biblical statements like this one from James as a basis for a radical withdrawal from the "world." But withdrawal is not the answer. Although it is true that we are called to be in the world but not "of the world" (John 17:14), we should love the people in this world enough to give them the gospel. To do so, we need to befriend them without befriending the things of this world that are opposed to God (see 1 John 3:15-17).

It is those who have responded to the call of Christ, who have believed in him, who are described as his friends (see John 15:9-17). It is interesting that in that same context Jesus spoke of the world's hatred: "If the world hates you, keep in mind that it hated me first" (John 15:18 NIV). Real friendship with God will frequently create a sense of alienation from the world. But we are not here as consumers, users, or pleasure-mad tourists. We are ambassadors, agents representing the King. We enter our world sponsored by him, equipped to carry out his work and promote his interests.

Anyone who chooses.NIV Because the world and God are pictured as enemies in this scene, choosing for one also means choosing against the other. People who choose friendship with the world also choose to become God's enemies—no one can serve two masters (Matthew 6:24). For those who are unwilling to accept this indictment, James has a serious question.

4:5 **Or do you think Scripture says without reason.**[NIV] Of course they don't think Scripture says anything without reason, so James reminds them what Scripture says.' James does not hesitate to call his readers to accountability before the whole of Scripture. What we say and teach must be rooted in God's Word. When our applications are challenged, we must be able to demonstrate that they flow from the principles and truth in the Bible.

The spirit he caused to live in us envies intensely.[NIV] James 4:6 (the next verse) is a quotation from the Old Testament—namely, Proverbs 3:34. However, this expression is not a direct quotation of any verse in the Old Testament. James is following an approach used elsewhere in the New Testament of summarizing Old Testament teaching rather than quoting directly (see, for instance, John 7:38; 1 Corinthians 2:9; Ephesians 5:14). Perhaps James has drawn from passages such as Exodus 20:5; 34:14; Zechariah 8:2. The phrase can be translated in several different ways (the NIV margin lists two other possibilities: "God jealously longs for the spirit that he made to live in us" and "The Spirit he caused to live in us longs jealously"). When the Greek text itself offers several alternative renderings, the context must help us determine what the original writer meant. Either James was saying that God, who caused his Spirit to dwell in the believers, is jealous for their friendship, or he was saying that the spirit that God put in man is one prone to jealousy—and therefore must be kept in check. The point of the statement is to affirm the believers' friendship with God over against the world.

We may say that we will befriend both God and the world, but in practice, we can only choose one way. The more we give ourselves to the world, the stronger will be our allegiance to the world. The more we give ourselves to God, the stronger will be our bond with him. "For where your treasure is, there your heart will be also" (Matthew 6:21 NRSV), said Jesus.

God has made us to be "one-track" people; it is our tendency toward sin that persuades us that we can be both loyal to God and still follow our own whims. This is the most destructive compromise a human being can make. It is exactly the same compromise Eve made when she accepted the idea that she could disobey God and keep an intimate relationship with him (see

Genesis 3:1-7). Such a compromise puts us on a track headed away from God.

To those who make the wise choice, facing what may seem like a hopeless battle, James adds a wonderful word of hope.

WHAT FEEDS OUR ENVY?

- Focusing on what others have
- Noticing what we don't have
- Allowing advertising to dictate our wants list
- Forgetting the basis for real contentment: peace with God and love of friends and family
- Being ungrateful for what we do have

4:6 He gives more grace.^{NKJV} This is a quotation of Proverbs 3:34. James uses it to offer hope to those who desire friendship with God. We will need to rely on God's grace to meet his standard. That grace is available. God demands loyalty and requires that his people resist the appeal of the evil world, but he gives grace that allows us to meet his demands.

Grace is God's help that we don't deserve. It is greater (which is what *more* literally means) than our need and more than we ask. No matter how heavy the awareness of our sinfulness or failure, God's grace is able to lift that burden with forgiveness. As Paul wrote, "But where sin increased, grace increased all the more" (Romans 5:20 NIV). But we cannot receive that grace until we realize that we need it and then humbly turn to God.

"God opposes the proud."^{NRSV} Pride makes us self-centered and leads us to conclude that we deserve all we can see, touch, or imagine. It creates greedy appetites for far more than we need. Pride can subtly cause us to no longer see our sins or our need for forgiveness. But humility opens the way for God's grace to flow into our lives.

Opposes is a military term for an enemy's actions. Part of the battle that James mentioned in James 4:1 is God's resistance to our evil desires. The inner turmoil is not just a conflict among our desires; it is also God waging war on our rebellious selves. By denying our prideful objectives, God is often able to get our attention. Times of frustration are important opportunities to

God gives what the demands.	*Augustine*

God is also merciful, gracious, all-loving and willingly supplies all that we need to meet his all-encompassing demands. *Doug Moo*

consider whether the goals we are pursuing are honoring to God or simply our own desires. Failure may be God's way of calling us back to friendship with him.

"But gives grace to the humble." The cure for evil desires is humility (see Proverbs 16:18-19; 1 Peter 5:5-6). What is this grace that God gives? By God's unmerited favor, the humble can have these special benefits: (1) They are in a position to enjoy a personal relationship with God based on the infinite merit of Christ, whose death created this position of acceptance they freely step into. (2) They have the privileges of access to God in prayer, daily fellowship with Christ, guidance by God's Spirit, a future hope in heaven, and the profound sense of being loved by God. Christ's death guaranteed these privileges. (3) They have the power of knowing that God is for them and nothing that comes against them can overcome him. Christ's resurrection demonstrated that power. The key to our own participation in these benefits depends on our willingness to be humble before God.

Humility is not weakness; instead, it is the only place that believers gain courage to face all their temptations and sins with God's strength. As God gives us more grace, we realize that this world's seductive attractions are only cheap substitutes for what God has to offer. It is our choice—we can humble ourselves and receive God's grace, or we can continue in our pride and self-sufficiency and experience his anger.

How do we, so prone to pride at the very moments when we think we might be approaching humility, discover true humility? How do we become the kind of humble people who find the overflowing grace that God promises? Having revealed our need, James now points clearly to the way.

Such grace is costly because it calls us to follow, and it is grace because it calls us to follow Jesus Christ. It is costly because it costs a man his life, and it is grace because it gives a man the only true life. It is costly because it condemns sin, and grace because it justifies the sinner. Above all, it is costly because it cost God the life of his Son: "ye were bought at a price," and what has cost God much cannot be cheap for us. Above all, it is grace because God did not reckon his Son too dear a price to pay for our life, but delivered him up for us.

Dietrich Bonhoeffer

WHAT IS GRACE?

By God's unmerited favor, I can have a daily relationship with him. This relationship is not something I can earn because it is based on Christ's infinite merit, not my own. Nor can I do anything to gain God's approval or cause him to love me more. God has reached down to my envious, loveless, rebellious heart and replaced it with Christ's own so that I am enabled to live for him.

4:7 Submit to God. NKJV Next James introduces a series of commands that both require and strengthen humility as we obey them. Humility is among the qualities that we simply cannot pursue directly. It, along with such traits as self-control, patience, endurance, peace, and joy, is a by-product of living God's way. In obedience we exercise what little humility we have. As we obey and become confident that obedience is the best way, humility will develop without our conscious attention. In fact, the less attention we give our own humility, the more likely we are to keep it.

[The devil] cannot dominate the servants of God who hope in him with all their hearts. The devil can wrestle, but he cannot pin. If, then, you resist him, he will flee defeated from you in disgrace. *Hermas*

HOW TO ENCOURAGE HUMILITY

When we discover humility in others, we actually do them a disservice in pointing it out. Saying to someone, "You are such a humble person," is not encouragement as much as it is tempting them to pride. We can better appreciate and encourage humility in others by expressing to them the impact of their obedience in a certain area. For example, if we note the humility of a person as they care for someone who the world would describe as "beneath them" on the social scale, we can simply say, "When I saw how you cared for that person, I was challenged by the more aware of the needs of people around me." Then we will be encouraging the action that demonstrated humility without spotlighting the humility itself.

We submit to God by recognizing both his friendship and his authority. We enter a relationship with God, not as equals, but as trusting servants. Friendship with God grows out of submission to him, not the other way around. Submission means that all we are and have is available to God without reservations. In the language of James, submission means that we consciously recognize God's desires ahead of our own. The word *submit* (*hupotagete*) literally means "be subject" in the sense that a soldier is expected to carry out the orders of his commanding officer. Submission is living a life that expresses to God, "Not my will, but yours be done." Submission is an act of the will assisted by God's Spirit.

Although he is not specifically defining the term, James is describing the life of faith. True faith responds to God actively rather than passively. Although God initiates and facilitates all that occurs between us and him, our involvement is never entirely excluded. Personal submission to God is part of living faith.

Resist the devil and he will flee from you. Although our own evil tendencies (1:14) and the desires battling within us (4:1) are the immediate sources of our problems, to give in to those internal desires is to yield to the devil (see Matthew 4:1-11; Luke 22:31; John 13:2, 27). Satan knows that as long as he can stimulate human pride, he can delay God's plan, even if only temporarily. But as powerful as Satan is, his only power over believers is in his powerful temptations. The devil can be resisted—and our resistance will cause him to flee. Conversely, a lack of resistance will practically guarantee ongoing harassment by Satan (see also Ephesians 6:10-18 and 1 Peter 5:6-9).

Once we have identified the devil as our enemy, we need to understand who he is and how he operates in order to effectively resist him. In the Bible, the names "devil" and "Satan" identify the same evil being (see Revelation 20:2). He is identified as the leader of angelic beings who revolted against God and were banished from heaven. The devil's primary purpose now is to separate man from God. Destined for destruction, he wants to take as much of creation with him as he possibly can. Among the reasons we so desperately need God's grace is that we are locked in mortal combat with a superior enemy. We need God's help to resist Satan's separating schemes and instead draw near to God. We must realize that the devil's power over us is only as strong as the illusion that he is more powerful than God's help. We must trust that "the one who is in you is greater than the one who is in the world" (1 John 4:4 NIV).

The devil's tools are seductions of many kinds. He tried three of them on Jesus (Matthew 4:1-11):

1. the seduction of self-sufficiency (challenging Jesus to meet his own needs)

2. the seduction of self-importance (challenging Jesus to test God)

3. the seduction of power (challenging Jesus to exchange power over the world for submission to the devil)

TACTICS AND WEAPONS FOR RESISTING THE DEVIL

We are commanded to "resist" the devil, to take a stand against him, now! Those intent on submitting to God ask, "now?"

TACTICS

God has not left us without battle plans. Here are some of his instructions:

Refuse to accept Satan's suggestion that we can be separated from Christ.

Romans 8:38-39

Ignore the temptation to doubt God's grace.

1 John 3:19-24

Reject the lie that we are beyond forgiveness.

1 John 1:9

Pray before, during, and after attacks by the devil.

Philippians 4:4-7
1 Thessalonians 5:16-24
James 1:2-8

Allow Christ to replace our way of thinking with his way of thinking.

Philippians 2:5-8; 4:8-9
Romans 12:1-2

WEAPONS

While the devil employs weapons of terror and illusion, God equips us with weapons of real power. They are only ineffective when we leave them unused. Among them are:

The belt of truth—wherever the truth is spoken and lived, the devil is unwelcome.

Ephesians 6:14
John 8:32; 14:6; 17:17

The breastplate of righteousness—living rightly is the result of advanced training in the faith. When we are living under God's guidance we are on guard against the devil's attacks.

Ephesians 6:14
Hebrews 5:12-14
1 Peter 2:12

The footwear of the gospel of peace—communicating the gospel is taking back territory controlled by the devil.

Ephesians 6:15
Matthew 24:14
Romans 1:16

The shield of faith—our faith in Christ makes him our shield and protector.	Ephesians 6:16 Hebrews 11:1 1 Peter 1:3-5
The helmet of salvation—the salvation that God offers is our eternal protection.	Ephesians 6:17 1 Thessalonians 5:8-9 Romans 1:16
The sword of the Spirit, God's Word—the Bible is a weapon when its truth is put to use, exposing the devil's work and helping those who are losing the battle.	Ephesians 6:17 2 Timothy 3:16 Hebrews 4:12
Prayer—in prayer we rely on God's help.	Ephesians 6:18-20 Hebrews 4:16 James 5:13-16

Behind each was the devil's attempt to get Jesus to doubt his relationship to God ("if you are the Son of God"). Among others that can be illustrated from James's letter are:

- the seduction to respond with bitterness to the hardships of life (1:2)

- the seduction to doubt persistently (1:6-8)

- the seduction to blame God for temptation (1:13-15)

- the seduction that good things come from someone other than God (1:16-18)

- the seduction that we can have faith without changing the way we live (1:22-25)

And those are only selections from the first chapter. The devil's arsenal is impressive. Even more, it is deadly deceptive.

As Paul wrote, "For though we live in the world, we do not wage war as the world does. The weapons we fight with are not the weapons of the world. On the contrary, they have divine power to demolish strongholds. We demolish arguments and every pretension that sets itself up against the knowledge of God, and we take captive every thought to make it obedient to Christ" (2 Corinthians 10:3-5 NIV).

The commands that follow, and indeed the rest of this letter, are footnotes on the above two statements. Both submission to God and resistance toward the devil are required. Friendship with the first; war with the second. James goes on to reveal glimpses of the variety of ways that submission to God and war with the devil are carried into the events and relationships of life.

4:8 **Draw near to God and he will draw near to you.** NRSV Next, James clarifies, expands, and applies his two commands to submit to God and to resist the devil. This and the following phrases emphasize action—our part in responding to what God has done. In Hebrews 10:19-22 the writer uses the same imagery to picture the dynamics of our relationship with God: "Let us draw near to God with a sincere heart in full assurance of faith, having our hearts sprinkled to cleanse us from a guilty conscience and having our bodies washed with pure water" (v. 22 NIV). Hebrews describes the old system, where God was separated from the people in the Holy of Holies, in the temple, by a curtain. But Christ provided a way through the curtain by his own body so that we might approach God without fear. We do not have to come very far when we come near, but we do have to come. The idea of submission now includes the added benefit of God's immediate response. As we submit our wills and desires to God, we will discover his care and closeness in ways we cannot perceive when we are in rebellion against him.

In order for some to act out their decision to come near to God, it is helpful to participate in some physical movement towards God. It may mean returning to church after an absence. It may involve continuing to attend church, but with a new sense of encountering God in worship. Others may need to make a public declaration within the church of their decision to draw near to God. These are not substitutes for the inward action of seeking God, but they can help confirm our intention.

Cleanse your hands, you sinners. NKJV The command to wash hands means to purify our actions and change our external behavior. The connection of washing to submission can be seen in the account of the Last Supper, where Jesus washed his disciples' feet. They had to submit to his serving them, which Peter found difficult to do (see John 13:3-10). The picture, then, involves the submission of our exterior lives to God's cleansing. The way we live matters to God.

As we submit or draw near to God, we will become aware of habits and actions in our lives that are not pleasing to him. Washing our hands pictures the removal of these things from the way we live. We must distance ourselves from the sins that God points out.

Purify your hearts, you double-minded. Similarly, the command to purify hearts calls for purity of thoughts and motives—

changes on the inside. It was not an option for the people to remain double-minded, trying to love both God and the world. If we allow the world to entice us away from God, we too have become "double-minded." James has already used this term in 1:8. There it refers to someone who can't decide if God is reliable. Here it refers to someone who is trying to maintain a friendship with both God and the world. Purity of heart, then, implies single-mindedness.

HOW DO WE PURIFY OUR HEARTS?

The Bible explains purifying our hearts as an act of submission to a cleansing that we cannot achieve on our own. John reminds us that "the blood of Jesus, his Son, purifies us from all sin" (1 John 1:7 NIV). The writer of Hebrews points this cleansing directly to our hearts and minds by telling us, "How much more, then, will the blood of Christ, who through the eternal Spirit offered himself unblemished to God, cleanse our consciences from acts that lead to death, so that we may serve the living God!" (Hebrews 9:14 NIV). Both internal and external cleansing are made possible by Christ's sacrifice on our behalf. We submit to the washing by asking God to make us clean. We pray like David, "Cleanse me with hyssop, and I will be clean; wash me, and I will be whiter than snow" (Psalm 51:7 NIV).

4:9 Lament and mourn and weep.[NRSV] Submission to God brings people to a new awareness of their condition and shortcomings. As God draws near to us, we ought to sense our unworthiness. After all, we are being allowed to approach the holy, perfect God. James has described a long spiritual process in the last eight verses. He began by describing people in conflict with each other and within themselves. Then he described the source of those conflicts as inappropriate desires motivated in large part by trying to stay close to the world and to God. Unmasking such a life and calling believers to submission may not be a welcome message. Surrender may not come easy. Long-held desires may respond with defiance. Repentance may have to include remembering how far we have broken from God's way before we have turned back.

These different terms, *lament*, *mourn*, and *weep*, capture the struggle of a soul drawing near to God. There is a dying which takes place. Paul invites us to consider ourselves "dead to sin, but alive to God in Christ Jesus" (Romans 6:11 NRSV). Today, few gospel preachers tell their listeners that they must forsake their selfish ways and surrender their lives to Jesus. Instead, they hear about turning to Christ as if it somehow did not involve the rather painful turning away from something or someone else.

Let your laughter be turned to mourning and your joy to gloom. NKJV This is a call to deep and heartfelt repentance. The people's laughter (scornful laughter that refuses to take sin seriously) and their enjoyment of the world's pleasures need to be completely changed—to mourning and gloom over their sins (see also Luke 6:25). Until this happens, there is no room for the laughter of real freedom and the joy of the Lord. The Christian life involves joy—but when we realize our sins, we must be mournful so that we can repent. Only after mourning can we move on to joy in the grace God gives us.

The sorrow being described in this verse is not a public show. We should not attempt to impress God with elaborate displays of repentance. There may be a time of public confession, but the grief-work over sin is largely private and interior. The presence of close friends may help, for sometimes they know us better than we know ourselves. They can also hold us accountable to our confession. But the outcome of this entire process must result in submission to God. The promises of his coming near (4:8), or of his lifting us up (4:10) are sure, but they can only be perceived by those who have humbled themselves before God. It is to this last picture of submission that James now turns.

4:10 Humble yourselves before the Lord. NRSV Echoing the Old Testament words from verse 6, that God gives grace to the humble, James tells his readers to humble themselves before God. God exalts those who humble themselves (Job 22:29; Proverbs 29:23; Isaiah 57:15; Matthew 23:12; Luke 14:11; 18:14; Philippians 2:5-11; 1 Peter 5:6). The picture gives us a helpful definition of God's grace: it is God lifting up those who have humbled themselves before him.

Humbling ourselves means recognizing that our worth comes from God alone. It is recognizing our desperate need for his help and submitting to his will for our lives. Although we do not deserve God's favor, he reaches out to us in love and gives us worth and dignity, despite our human shortcomings. According to Luke 18 (NIV), when Jesus noted those around him who were "confident of their own righteousness and looked down on everybody else" (v.9), he told the parable of the Pharisee and the tax collector who found themselves together in the temple praying. The contrast between the two men challenges the tendency we have towards self-righteousness. The Pharisee "prayed about himself" (v.11), while the tax collector humbled himself and prayed, "God, have mercy on me, a sinner" (v.13). Jesus pointed out that only the tax collector returned home "justified before God" (v.14). Jesus' summary was, "Everyone who exalts himself will be humbled, and he who humbles himself will be exalted" (v.14).

He will lift you up. NKJV One of the most touching biblical illustrations of this truth is found in Jesus' parable of the forgiving father (see Luke 15:11–32). The son took his inheritance and set out to be the world's best friend. It was not until he found himself bankrupt in every way that he repented. He returned home, grieving. The son confessed to his father that he was unworthy to be called a son. But the father lifted him up and welcomed him back into the family. The act of returning required submission. The wayward son's words of repentance required humility. The end result was great joy. Humility before God will be followed by his lifting us up.

WHY IS IT SO DIFFICULT TO SUBMIT TO GOD?
- Self-reliance and independence are strong cultural values.
- The systems of advertising and entertainment promote our self-reliance and independence.
- Humility is a trait discouraged and ridiculed in the media.
- All of this reinforces our natural tendency toward selfishness.

4:11   Do not speak evil of one another. NKJV With an abrupt shift from describing an appropriate attitude towards God, James turns to the proper relations between brothers. The sequence reminds us of the great commandment, "'Love the Lord your God with all your heart and with all your soul and with all your mind.' This is the first and greatest commandment. And the second is like it: 'Love your neighbor as yourself'" (Matthew 22:37-39 NIV). We love God by submitting to him; we love our neighbor by refusing to speak evil. James applies Jesus' words to the problems among the Christians to whom he was writing.

Verses 11 and 12 form the conclusion to 3:1–4:12. With respect to the improper use of the tongue as described in 3:1-12, James was probably referring specifically to slander and judgment. It seems that James's readers were having a tremendous problem with dissension because certain individuals (undoubtedly leaders, in light of 3:1) were slandering each other and causing tremendous problems in the church.

The Greek word translated *speak evil* (*katalaleite*) refers to any form of speaking evil against a person. To slander means to make false charges in order to damage a person's reputation. But the term as used here is broader than that. We may speak the truth about a person and still be unkind, or we may spread gossip that others have no business knowing. We may be questioning someone's authority or nullifying their good work by backbiting. Obviously, this hurts the harmony among believers (see also Romans 1:29-30; 2 Corinthians 12:20; 1 Peter 2:1). The tense in the Greek reveals that James is forbidding a practice that is already in progress. The people were in the habit of criticizing one another.

SILENCING SLANDER
To silence slander we must regularly examine our attitudes and actions toward others. Do we build people up or tear them down? When we are ready to criticize someone, we ought to remember God's law of love and say something good instead. Saying something beneficial to others will cure us of finding fault and increase our ability to obey God's law of love. For those immersed in a culture that thrives on criticism and slander, Jesus set a standard to guide each of us: "I tell you, forgive your brother not seven times, but seventy-seven times" (Matthew 18:22 NIV). One practical approach to silencing a slandering habit is to practice making seven positive, encouraging statements for every critical one we make.

Anyone who speaks against his brother or judges him speaks against the law and judges it. NIV This verse includes the sixth and seventh times in his letter that James has mentioned the law (see 1:25; 2:8-10, 12). It is the royal law—the law that frees or convicts, the law that must be kept. Here the law is under attack. The specific problem being confronted violates the ninth commandment: "You shall not bear false witness against your neighbor" (Exodus 20:16 NRSV). It also violates the more fundamental law of Christ, "Love your neighbor as yourself" (Matthew 22:39; see also Leviticus 19:18). Jesus called this the second greatest commandment (Mark 12:31) and illustrated it when he said, "Do to others what you would have them do to you" (Matthew 7:12 NIV). If a believer speaks against another believer, he is disobeying this law because he is not showing love and is not treating others as he would like to be treated. His disobedience shows disregard for the law, for he is passing judgment on its validity, or "sitting in judgment on it" (NIV). By doing so, he is putting himself above God. When we judge one another in this slanderous way, we are clearly failing to submit to God.

If you judge the law, you are not a doer of the law. NKJV/NRSV The gospel does not invalidate the law. Those in Christ are not free to break the commandments because we live "under grace." God's commandments that reveal our inability to live perfectly become, for believers, guidelines about the kind of life God wants us to live. Disobeying the commandments is still sin, whether a person is a believer or not. Obeying the commandments is one way to thank God for relieving us of the hopeless duty of trying to obtain our salvation through them. It is also one of the clear ways to demonstrate submission to God.

4:12 One Lawgiver and Judge.^{NIV} God is both the source and enforcer of the law. We who are accountable to God's law cannot place ourselves in God's place. Our rightful role is to keep the law, not use it as a weapon on others, or treat it as worthless. Behind the law is the awesome and holy God. The only safe way into his presence is the way of humble submission, not arrogance.

Who is able to save and destroy. God rewards those who obey the law and destroys those who disobey (see Deuteronomy 32:39; 1 Samuel 2:6; Psalm 68:20; 75:6-7; Matthew 10:28).

Who are you to judge another?^{NKJV} James takes away any rights we might claim for criticizing our neighbors. Behind the critical spirit is an attitude that usurps God's authority and is full of pride. There should be no critical, harsh faultfinding in the body of Christ. Romans 14:4 says, "Who are you to judge someone else's servant? To his own master he stands or falls. And he will stand, for the Lord is able to make him stand" (NIV).

> There are no ordinary people. You have never talked to a mere mortal. Nations, cultures, arts, civilizations—these are mortal, and their life is to ours as the life of a gnat. But it is immortals whom we joke with, work with, marry, snub, and exploit—immortal horrors or everlasting splendors. *C. S. Lewis*

WHO ARE YOU, INDEED?
It is the height of arrogance to judge others because the right to judge belongs only to God. So the person who judges assumes God's role. Before passing sentence on others we ought to look in the mirror of our own identity. There we will find:

- sin
- shortcomings
- guilt for the very failure we see in others
- personal need for God's grace and mercy

The principle in this verse does not prohibit the proper action of a church against a member who is acting in flagrant disobedience to God (1 Corinthians 5–6). Rather, James is concerned with the critical speech that condemns or judges others' actions and their standing with God. He is confronting individuals who might be tempted to set themselves up as personal watchdogs over other believers.

We might think that just criticizing a church member or spreading a little interesting gossip is not that serious—especially when compared to other sins. But the Bible sees it as a sin of utmost seriousness because it breaks the law of love and it tries to usurp God's authority. As we saw in chapter 3, the tongue is a tool of deadly sin. We dare not minimize its danger.

A PRAYER OF SUBMISSION TO THE ROYAL LAW
It is helpful to examine in prayer how well we are doing at loving our neighbor as we love ourselves. We can ask God to help us examine our way. Several questions to ask are:

■ Have I given myself the benefit of the doubt, but refused it to my brother or sister?

■ Have I made excuses for my shortcomings, but remained intolerant of others?

■ Have I judged my brothers and sisters according to the letter of the law while expecting grace for myself?

TRUST GOD IN MAKING PLANS / 4:13-17

James maintains the passion of the last section in this new one. The progression has moved from submitting ourselves and our relationships to God, to our future and the need to entrust it to God.

This section includes three essential facts of life that make for good planning:

(1) God is in control—"If it is the Lord's will" (4:15)

(2) Life is a daily gift—"we will live" (4:15)

(3) All our going and doing must be carried out with the first two points in mind.

This section is not an argument against making careful plans; rather, it is a caution to submit to God, even in our planning.

4:13 Listen, you who say, "Today or tomorrow we will . . ."[NIV] The *you* is most likely businesspeople. Addressing this letter to scattered people presumes, at least in part, people moving to establish new lives in distant places. The last paragraph dealt with the spiritual dangers facing those who do not travel. This section deals with those who travel abroad. But its lessons apply to any situation that requires planning. *Listen* (see also 5:1) carries the Old Testament connotation of divine judgment that's *imminent*. It expresses disapproval and warning to those who disregard it.

Business travel for selling and trading was common in the first century, especially among Jews—for example, Priscilla and Aquila (Acts 18:2, 18; Romans 16:3) and Lydia (Acts 16:14). Planning is not evil—in fact, businesspeople are wise to plan ahead. Traveling merchants make travel plans—to leave when a ship or caravan is ready, to buy and sell their goods, to probably stay a year, and to return with a profit. They plan in specific detail. The problem that James addresses, however, is that God is not included in those plans. The merchants plan with arrogance, thinking they can go wherever they like and stay for as long as they like. Their way of planning, doing business, and using money may be honest, but it is really no different than the planning of any pagan businessperson. These Christian businesspeople ought to know better.

James is not even questioning the profit motive in the plans of these brothers and sisters. He is simply confronting that easy progression of living without consideration for God. Terms like self-assertiveness, self-confidence, and self-centeredness may have some limited usefulness, but they also describe attitudes that can ignore God. Yet God owns us and all our business.

PRACTICAL ATHEISTS

Many people say they believe in God, but, in reality, they are practical atheists. That is, in the way they make decisions and plan for the future, they live as if God didn't exist. They take no account of God's sustaining care or common grace; they act as if they are self-sufficient and in control; and they take credit for all the good they experience. Listening to these people speak, we would have no idea that God is a factor in their lives. How much better it is to actively recognize God's right to order and direct our lives as he pleases. Self-reliance and independence rightfully belong to God alone. Why do believers and even churches so often want to take matters into their own hands? When do *you* tend to leave God out of the picture?

The fact is that God has a prior claim on our lives. First, because he is our Creator, his purposes can demand precedence over our priorities. Second, for believers, this claim is reenforced by the knowledge that we no longer belong to ourselves: "You are not your own; you were bought at a price" (1 Corinthians 6:19-20 NIV). God's claim on us is both as Creator and Savior. Our submission to God must be expressed in every area of our lives.

LEAVING GOD OUT

Here are some common ways that we talk about the future and make our plans, while leaving God out:

- When we describe retirement in selfish terms as our time to enjoy the fruits of our labors
- When we see work and careers as ways we can make money in order to buy what we want
- When we define money as a symbol of independence
- When we imagine ourselves in control of major areas of life under the rationalization that God is not interested in such mundane matters
- When we make practical decisions about education, job changes, moving, investments, and spending—all without prayer

GOD'S WILL AND OUR PLANS

It is good to have goals, but goals can disappoint us if we leave God out of them. There is no point in making plans as though God does not exist because the future is in his hands. The beginning of good planning is to ask: "What would I like to be doing ten years from now? One year from now? Tomorrow? How will I react if God steps in and rearranges my plans?" We can plan ahead, but we must hold on to our plans loosely. If we put God's desires at the center of our planning, he will never disappoint us.

4:14 **You do not even know what tomorrow will bring.** ᴺᴿˢⱽ There is a problem with these well-made plans—no one can know what will happen tomorrow, to say nothing of a year in the future (see Proverbs 27:1; Luke 12:16-21). These people were planning as if their future was guaranteed. James is not suggesting that they make no plans because of possible disaster, but to be realistic about the future as they trust God to guide them. Because the future is uncertain, it is even more important that we completely depend on God. The plans for our lives need to include frequent self-reminders about God's role in the future. One helpful, traditional prayer is: "Lord, I know I don't know what the future holds, but I'm glad I know you hold the future!" Our attitude on any particular day must never leave us open to the response God gave the rich man in Jesus' parable, "You fool! This very night your life is being demanded of you" (Luke 12:20 NRSV).

What is your life? You are a mist.[NIV] James illustrates his point that our lives are uncertain by comparing them to a fog that covers the countryside in the morning and then is burned away by the sun. Life is short no matter how long we live. We shouldn't be deceived into thinking we have plenty of time left to live for Christ, to enjoy our loved ones, or to do what we know we should. Today is the day to live for God! Then, no matter when our lives end, we will have fulfilled God's plans for us.

Realizing the future is uncertain not only teaches us trust in God, it helps us to properly value the present. To be obsessed with future plans may work our failure to appreciate present blessings or our evasion of present duties. *John Wesley*

PARTNERSHIP WITH GOD

God is the senior partner in any business we pursue. The following questions will keep our business in line with God's priorities:

- *Purpose*—Does our mission ultimately serve God and the people he created? Does it practice harmony with his creation?
- *Philosophy*—Do our business practices and principles treat people with dignity? Are they ethical, caring, and compassionate? Are there examples of good stewardship of resources?
- *Plan*—Do our daily activities and attitudes show clear evidence of the Christian life? Do we consult the Bible for constant input to our decisions?

4:15 You ought to say, "If the Lord wills . . ."[NKJV] Believers cannot live independently of God; therefore, our plans cannot ignore him. We must make sure those plans include the clause, *if the Lord wills*. We are to plan, but we are to recognize God's higher will and divine sovereignty.

James began this chapter by exposing the danger of our uncontrolled desires. We are prone to demand our will. The way out of danger involves submission of our wills to God, so that our attitude becomes more and more in line with the Lord's will. We exchange our desires for his desires. Then we discover, to our great delight, that those things that we rightly desired are granted after all, only now there is no doubt that God has been the provider. Jesus said, "But seek first his kingdom and his righteousness, and all these things will be given to you as well" (Matthew 6:33 NIV). The kingdom of God and his righteousness exist anywhere that God's will is being carried out.

This means far more than simply saying, "If God wills,"

whenever we speak about future plans, for that too can become meaningless. It means planning *with* God as we make our plans. Our plans should be evaluated by God's standards and goals, and they should be prayed over with time spent listening for God's advice. Such planning pleases God.

4:16 You boast and brag. All such boasting is evil. NIV These businesspeople, instead of focusing on God's will in their plans, were arrogantly boasting as though they could control their own destiny. Such boasting is evil because it takes no thought of God.

The most dangerous moments in life occur when a plan we have engineered succeeds. That moment of satisfaction can more easily become pride than it can become humility. But the Bible illustrates the truth that even our greatest successes ought to be submitted to God. Daniel recounts vividly the story of King Nebuchadnezzar's moment of success. His reflection was entirely self-centered: "He said, 'Is not this the great Babylon I have built as the royal residence, by my mighty power and for the glory of my majesty?'" (Daniel 4:30 NIV). Daniel had warned the king that pride would be his downfall. The prophecy was fulfilled exactly: "Immediately what had been said about Nebuchadnezzar was fulfilled. He was driven away from people and ate grass like cattle. His body was drenched with the dew of heaven until his hair grew like the feathers of an eagle and his nails like the claws of a bird" (Daniel 4:33 NIV). The king was humbled. When he was finally restored, his reflection had a distinctly different tone: "Now I, Nebuchadnezzar, praise and exalt and glorify the King of heaven, because everything he does is right and all his ways are just. And those who walk in pride he is able to humble" (Daniel 4:37 NIV).

HUMILITY—ONE WAY OR ANOTHER
The choice is inevitable. Either we humble ourselves before God, or we will be humbled. That humbling may not be immediate, but it is guaranteed. It will come at that time when all people, joyfully or not, will recognize God's right to our submission. Everyone will recognize God's authority when "at the name of Jesus every knee should bend, in heaven and on earth and under the earth, and every tongue should confess that Jesus Christ is Lord, to the glory of God the Father" (Philippians 2:10-11 NRSV).

4:17 Anyone, then, who knows the right thing to do and fails to do it, commits sin. NRSV Verse 17 sums up all of chapters 1–4. It sums up the entire ethical problem in the whole Epistle of James. He may be telling these merchants that they know what they should do—that is, honor God in their business practices. If they ignore that, they sin. In a broader sense, James adds these words as an admonition for all his readers to do what he has written. They have been told, so they have no excuse.

We tend to limit sins to specific acts—*doing* wrong. But James tells us that sin is also *not* doing what is right. (These two kinds of sin are sometimes called sins of commission and sins of omission.) It is a sin to lie; it can also be a sin to know the truth and not tell it. It is a sin to speak evil of someone; it is also a sin to avoid that person when you know he needs your friendship. We should be willing to help others as the Holy Spirit guides us. If God has directed you to do a kind act, to render a service to others, or to restore a relationship—do it. You will experience a renewed and refreshed vitality to your Christian faith.

REAL GOOD BUSINESS

It is unfortunate that the term "good business" has so little to do with goodness in the world today. Many would say that business cannot survive and the people in business do good at the same time. Good business, then, is whatever is good for the business, not necessarily what is good for those with whom we are doing business. James's simple response would probably be, "Expect those who are the world's friends to act that way. But if you claim to love God, you will have to conduct business by his standards. You must do good!"

Here are specific areas where a business can practice good toward its employees and those it serves:

- Provide a peaceful place to work
- Give fair wages for the work
- Confront, defuse, and settle disputes and quarrels
- Exemplify humility in leadership
- Practice Christian values of honesty, integrity, and faithfulness
- Compete in the marketplace without falsehood or deception

James 5

WARNING TO THE RICH / 5:1-6

After taking a deep breath, James turns his attention to the rich. They have been hovering in the background throughout this letter. Chapter 1 included the challenge to see that humble circumstances have distinct spiritual benefits (see 1:9-11) as opposed to riches, which require humility. In chapter 2, James warned about the destructiveness of preferential treatment based on wealth. At the end of chapter 4, James warned against being seduced by the world. He begins chapter 5 by warning wealthy non-Christians of their hopeless end and the worthlessness of their riches. Their wealth will not save them from God's judgment. Their crimes include hoarding wealth, not paying their workers' wages, living in luxury and self-indulgence, and murdering innocent people. But they will not go unpunished. This should comfort the believers, knowing that any wrongs against them will be avenged. It should also be a clear warning that they shouldn't make riches the focus of their desires because, ultimately, riches amount to nothing.

Does James care what happens to the rich? If he didn't, he would be violating his own forceful statements about the law to love one's neighbor. Being rich doesn't make someone a non-neighbor.

5:1 Now listen.[NIV] James has followed his appeal for submission to God with helpful applications of the principle to several different groups. In 4:11-12, submission to God means that brothers do not verbally abuse one another. In 4:13-16, submission to God means that our future plans are made with humility. In 4:17, submission to God means that failing to do what we know God wants us to do is sin. Here James turns his attention to a group even farther from the truth.

> James . . . has a regard to the faithful, that they, hearing of the miserable end of the rich, might not envy their fortune, and also that knowing that God would be the avenger of the wrongs they suffered, they might bear with a calm and resigned mind bear them.   *John Calvin*

MONEY: WHAT DOES GOD SAY?

DANGERS OF MONEY	Forgetting God	Deuteronomy 6:10-13; 8:11-20 Proverbs 18:11 Luke 18:24
	Acting dishonestly, taking advantage of others	2 Kings 5:20-27 Proverbs 10:2; 22:16, 22-23 1 Timothy 6:9-10
	Being greedy	Isaiah 5:8-9 Amos 3:10; 5:11; 8:4-7 James 5:1-6
	Allowing it to take God's place	Exodus 20:17 Luke 12:15-21 Ephesians 5:5
ADVICE ABOUT MONEY	Give generously and cheerfully to help the poor	Proverbs 11:28; 18:11 Matthew 6:24 Luke 6:24
	Give generously to those doing God's work	Proverbs 11:24-25; 19:17; 21:13; 22:9; 28:27 Luke 12:33-34 2 Corinthians 9:7
	Get out and stay out of debt	Deuteronomy 25:4 Nehemiah 13:10-11 1 Timothy 5:17
	Tithe	Psalm 37:21 Proverbs 3:27-28; 22:7 Romans 13:8
	Don't cosign for another's debt	Malachi 3:8-10 1 Corinthians 16:2
	Don't accept bribes	Proverbs 11:15; 17:18; 22:26-27
	Pay your taxes	Exodus 23:8 Psalm 15:5 Proverbs 17:23
	Always be honest	Romans 13:6-7
	Provide for your family	Deuteronomy 25:14-16 Proverbs 20:10, 23 Luke 16:10-12
	Plan wisely for the future	1 Timothy 5:8
		Proverbs 21:20; 22:3; 24:3-4, 27, 27:23-27

CORRECT PERSPECTIVE ON MONEY	Everything comes from God	1 Chronicles 29:11-14 Colossians 1:15-17
	Money cannot buy salvation	Proverbs 11:4 Ezekiel 7:19 Matthew 16:26 Luke 16:19-31; 18:18-25
	Riches do not last	James 1:10-11 Revelation 18:11-19
	Money never satisfies	Ecclesiastes 5:10-11 Luke 12:15
	Don't show favoritism to the rich	James 2:1-9
	Money carries responsibility	1 Timothy 6:17-19
	Obey God rather than chase after money	Psalm 119:36 Proverbs 19:1; Psalm 17:15
	Be content	Philippians 4:11-13 1 Timothy 6:8 Hebrews 13:5
A WORD TO EMPLOYERS	Pay wages in full and right away	Leviticus 19:13 Deuteronomy 24:14-15 Jeremiah 22:13 Malachi 3:5
	Severe judgment awaits employers who unfairly withhold wages	Amos 5:11; 8:4-7 James 5:1-6
	Be fair	Proverbs 11:26 Ephesians 6:9 Colossians 4:1

You rich people. NRSV These are probably not believers, but rich nonbelievers (perhaps the same people referred to in 2:6), for James does not hold out to them any immediate offer of deliverance as he does for sinning believers. Very likely the wealthy landowners are the objects of James's scathing rebuke.

Weep and wail for the miseries that are coming to you. NRSV No, these rich people are not in misery now—they have lavish surroundings, plenty of food, plenty of money. But misery is coming upon them—not earthly suffering, but eternal suffering— and they should be wailing in sorrow for what they will lose then. The words *weep* and *wail* were often used in the Old Testament by the prophets to describe the reaction of the wicked when the Day of the Lord (the day of God's judgment) arrives (see Isaiah 13:6; 15:3; Amos 8:3). Jesus said that those who would be excluded from God's kingdom would be weeping and gnashing their teeth (Matthew 8:12; 22:13; 24:51; 25:30).

While the rich are invited to weep and wail, we are *not* invited to gloat. In fact, gloating over their present repentance or future humiliation would be a backhanded admission that we are envious of their possessions. Before demanding justice from God, we must always check our motives. The descriptions of judgment that follow are prescriptions against desiring that lifestyle ourselves. The lustful desires for riches will be just as shamefully shattered as the riches themselves. Submission to God never allows us to move very far from repentance and humility.

As is the case with many passages in the Bible that deal with judgment on the mismanagement of wealth, the question of application is important. Frankly, most people, whatever their financial condition, will not easily claim the title of "rich." This is specially true when the context includes harsh criticism. If we claim not to be wealthy, then do we pay attention only to what God says about those who are oppressed? What if we are among neither the wealthy nor the oppressed? Does God allow us to know about his judgment just so that we can cheer with those who have been mistreated? Or does our knowledge of God's plans make us responsible to be careful of our allegiances? If we are members of a society where oppression is widely practiced, we may feel God's judgment even if we were not actively treating others unjustly. What James makes clear (see 2:1-7) is that believers need to be a force that combats oppression, treats oppressors with dignity but not deference, defends the rights of the oppressed, and treats them with respect. Whatever our posi-

The settled happiness and security which we all desire, God withholds from us by the very nature of the world: but joy, pleasure, and merriment he has scattered broadcast. We are never safe, but we have plenty of fun, and some ecstasy. It is not hard to see why. The security we crave would teach us to rest our hearts in this world and pose an obstacle to our return to God: a few moments of happy love, a landscape, a symphony, a merry meeting with our friends, a bath or a football match, have no such tendency. Our Father refreshes us on the journey with some pleasant inns, but will not encourage us to mistake them for home.

C. S. Lewis

tion on the financial scale, allegiance to Jesus Christ ought to make a difference in the way we live.

5:2 Your riches have rotted.^{NRSV} The instability of wealth is the clearest warning of the coming misery of the rich. Goods that rot and are ruined and possessions that break and rust all indicate the impermanence of life. God sends reminders along the way (sickness, death of others, disasters) that we need to find security in what is eternal. Misery will be the result of ignoring these indicators of impermanence. As he often does in this letter, James simply gives direct application of the teaching of Christ. Jesus said, "Do not store up for yourselves treasures on earth, where moth and rust destroy, and where thieves break in and steal. But store up for yourselves treasures in heaven, where moth and rust do not destroy, and where thieves do not break in and steal" (Matthew 6:19-20 NIV). The Greek word for *riches* (*ploutos*) is a general description of all that these rich people have. But their money, security, lavishness, and self-indulgence are as good as rotted because they can do nothing for them in eternity. In ancient times, wealth included, for the most part, hard goods such as food (as in crops), clothing, and precious metal. Some could be lost because it had become rotten.

Your clothes are moth-eaten.^{NRSV} These rich people hoarded even their clothing, not willing to give their excess to the poor. They had so many pieces of clothing (a luxury in those days), that before they were worn out, moth larvae had eaten them. Remember, this letter was addressed to people in a society where a poor man probably had only one cloak.

5:3 Gold and silver are corroded.^{NIV} Precious metals have been hoarded away, unused. When it is kept from being used to help others, wealth "corrodes"; in other words, it is wasted. Although silver and gold cannot actually corrode, they can tarnish, and the tarnish testifies to how long the gold and silver have been kept untouched. James warns us that even what seems most indestructible is doomed if it is not put to good use.

> He is no fool who gives up what he cannot keep to gain what he cannot lose.   *Jim Elliot*

Today, certain pieces of paper have great value: stocks, bonds, and future commodities. But all these valuable items are transitory. The market that makes a person wealthy one day robs him or her of everything the next. Inflation is not only an economic state, it is also a view of life that places too high a value on the things of this world. The greater the inflated value of things that are not lasting, the greater the disappointment at their loss. Jesus made very clear what the bottom line really is: "What good will it be for a man if he gains the whole world, yet forfeits his soul? Or what can a man give in exchange for his soul?" (Matthew 16:26 NIV). Compared to the values of the kingdom of God, the earth's most precious possessions fade away in tarnish and rust.

> God has not appointed gold for rust, nor garments for moths; but, on the contrary, he has designed them as aids and helps to human life. *John Calvin*

SAVING OR HOARDING?

In a consumer-oriented society, the benefits of saving are often lost in the quest for instant gratification, conspicuous wealth, and fearful hoarding. James's warnings are not against saving money. He is combating the kind of selfish hoarding that affects not only the person, but everyone else in that person's life.

Benefits of Saving	Dangers of Hoarding
■ Demonstrates good stewardship of resources provided by God	■ Fosters a sense of earthly security and independence from God
■ Makes a person able to respond to the needs of others	■ Promotes a sense of superiority over others
■ Assumes that God sometimes provides for people through other people	■ Assumes that what a person gains is only for that person's benefit
■ Is responsible preparation for tomorrow	■ Is irresponsible indulgence for today
■ Promotes wise spending decisions	■ Promotes impulsive spending decisions

Their corrosion will testify against you and eat your flesh like fire.NIV The uselessness of hoarded gold and silver will cover them like corrosion. It will be the irrefutable evidence that reveals the greed, selfishness, and wickedness of the rich. The truth and shame of that corrosion will burn like fire. The testimony of wealth hoarded selfishly will cause God's judgment to fall upon the wealthy, and they will be forever condemned to hell "where the fire never goes out" (Mark 9:43). They failed to do good with what they had, and that was sin (4:17). Their greed will destroy them.

Few people in the Western world can read this passage with understanding and not be at least singed by its truth. We have probably added a new dimension to the problem in that we have not hoarded in order to preserve for later; rather, we have hoarded in order to waste. Believers today find themselves participating in society's tendency to consume as much as possible without regard to the conditions elsewhere in the world, or even what we will leave to our children and grandchildren. Will not the corrosion of our accumulated waste testify against us also?

You have laid up treasure for the last days.

NRSV Jesus repeatedly warned that his return would be unexpected. His followers were to live in constant anticipation of his return. References to the last days were reminders of the Christian priorities. Their lives were to be spent doing what really mattered—serving Christ (see Mark 1:15; Acts 2:17; 2 Timothy 3:1; Hebrews 1:2). When the last days arrive, the hoarding will all be a waste. The rich will be caught with their hands full, but it will be an accumulation of nothing. These people will face God's wrath because they have chased after earthly treasure to the exclusion of treasure in heaven. Their hoarding will not only demonstrate their wrong priorities, it will also show how their actions deprived the needy of help and resources that could have been given. James has already pointed out that "judgment without mercy will be shown to anyone who has not been merciful" (2:13).

> Riches are the instrument of all vices, because they render us capable of putting even our worst desires into execution. *Ambrose*

ANTIDOTE TO HOARDING
To be prepared for the last days we should:
- Live in submission to God.
- Live in awareness of and response to God's grace.
- Live in sensitivity to the needs of others.
- Live to meet the needs of others.
- Live with a view toward eternity.

5:4 **The wages you failed to pay the workmen . . . are crying out against you.** NIV These workmen worked for rich people during the day and would be paid at the end of the day. They were poor peasants. Most likely they had been forced off their own land by foreclosures, and then they hired themselves out to the wealthy holder of a huge estate. They lived on the verge of starvation—today's wages bought tomorrow's food. If a worker did not receive his pay, his whole family went hungry. (Jesus' parable of the workers in the vineyard is a picture of this society; see Matthew 20:1-16.) If the owner refused to pay—either to hoard it until the end of the harvest in order to keep the workers coming back, just to be ornery, or to default completely—there was little or nothing the workman could do. Complaining might mean loss of a job and blacklisting, and he couldn't afford a lawyer. The money that should have gone to the workers is also evidence against these rich people.

This verse brings the weight of God's work ethic in the Bible to bear on the conditions that James is confronting. If these rich people are Jewish unbelievers, perhaps they will respond to the condemnations God consistently leveled against those who cheated in their business dealings (see Leviticus 19:13; Deuteronomy 24:14-15; Proverbs 3:27-28; Jeremiah 22:13; Malachi 3:5).

Both the withheld wages and the harvesters are crying out to God. This expression recalls God's response to the first act of injustice in Genesis 4:10: "The Lord said, 'What have you done? Listen! Your brother's blood cries out to me from the ground.'" Abel's blood cried out to God for justice. The picture emphasized God's awareness of injustice. It will not go unpunished.

The cries of the harvesters have reached the ears of the Lord of hosts. NRSV There was no excuse for lack of payment—these workmen had harvested heaps of grain that would be sold. But the rich were willing to let it rot rather than to even pay the workmen. The only resource the poor had was to call out to God, the Lord Almighty. This name for God is, literally, *Lord of Sabaoth;* it conveys the sense of awe, power, and majesty of the Creator. The supreme ruler will intercede for the poor. This name is used in Isaiah 5:9, also condemning the rich: "The LORD Almighty has declared in my hearing: 'Surely the great houses will become desolate, the fine mansions left without occupants'" (NIV). This is the almighty God who hears the cries of the poor (see also Psalm 17:1-6; 18:6; 31:2).

What are the implications of God being almighty or all-powerful? If we are facing oppression, faith requires that we remember God is our strength and our defender. Temporary circumstances do not change the fact of God's sovereignty. God will protect us from spiritual evil in this life and give us the joys we desire in the next. He will insure that justice will be done, and he will judge the oppressors.

5:5 You have lived on the earth. NRSV The rich must realize that everything they have is earthbound. Their reward is here and now; their judgment will come later.

Luxury and self-indulgence. NIV The lifestyles of the rich and famous may make interesting media fodder, but they are noxious to God. These rich, who have taken the land from the poor and then refused to pay their deserved wages, have shown gross lack of concern and selfishness. To this they have added an attitude of wastefulness and self-indulgence that God detests.

THE MARKS OF SELF-INDULGENCE

When our lives begin to display the following characteristics, we are practicing self-indulgence (see the parable of Lazarus and the rich man in Luke 16:19-31 for illustrations of many of these):

- When we assume that wealth should always be used first to meet our needs
- When we visualize wealth as a protection or insulation between us and the rest of the world
- When we waste, destroy, or discard what others could put to good use
- When we display smugness or pride at the differences between what we have and what others have
- When we invest in things purely for status without considering their usefulness

Terms such as *luxury* and *self-indulgence* invite us to defensiveness. The availability of resources and credit quickly have us redefining luxuries as necessities, and self-indulgences as perks or rewards. But following Christ means that our tendencies must be questioned. They also must be curbed. Rich people like the ones James was describing will not do this because they have not submitted to God. Our lack of discipline in these areas will indicate our need for submission also.

A life of luxury and self-indulgence is essentially worthless. Money will mean nothing when Christ returns, so we should spend our time accumulating treasures that will be worthwhile in God's eternal kingdom. Money itself is not the problem: Christian leaders need money to live and support their families; missionaries need money to do their work effectively. It is the *love* of money that leads to evil (1 Timothy 6:10) and causes some to oppress others to get more. This is a warning to all Christians who are tempted to adopt worldly standards rather than God's standards (Romans 12:1-2) and an encouragement to all those who are oppressed by the rich.

God is not against pleasure, entertainment, or beautiful things. But everything must be submitted to him. They are meant to be helps to others, ways to restore us for further work, bridges of contact with others, and hints reminding us that God has been very gracious to us.

Fattened your hearts in a day of slaughter.^{NRSV} Jesus said, "Where your treasure is, there your heart will be also" (Matthew

6:21). For these people, their treasure is worldly wealth, "fattened" in ways that were not just. They have enjoyed life, feasting as they would on the day when an animal is slaughtered. Ironically, James says that *they* are like fattened animals and that *they* will be slaughtered when the day of God's judgment arrives (see Jeremiah 12:1-3). Selfishness is a dangerous fattening of our hearts. Selfishness leads to judgment and destruction. (See Deuteronomy 6:10-12 for the dangers of prosperity.)

5:6 Condemned and murdered innocent men. These innocent men are believers, the poor workmen and harvesters mentioned in 5:4. This murder probably was both active and passive. Inconvenient people may indeed have been murdered; but more likely, the poor people who could not pay their debts were thrown in prison or forced to sell all their possessions. With no means of support and no opportunity even to work off their debts, these poor people and their families often died of starvation. God also considered this murder. Either way, in the unjust system, it was legal. The poor were defenseless (**were not opposing you**). Their only recourse against the evil rich was to cry out to God.

One of the marks of oppression is a dissatisfaction with merely abusing others or taking from them what is theirs. Oppression demonstrates its demonic origin in its goal to destroy those being used. James is confronting a mind-set that treats others without regard for their dignity, conspires to cheat them out of everything, defrauds them of possessions and wages, and disregards the very lives of those who have been mistreated.

There will always be organizations and institutions that allow this kind of oppression to exist legally. The rich will get richer. The poor will sink more deeply into poverty. But believers must know that God is passionately against oppression. Human law, as contrived as it sometimes is, does not determine right and wrong in God's eyes. Human law does not require charity or genuine concern for our neighbors. But God's law and God's character demand a higher order of living from us.

Christians can easily fall into this kind of sin by rationalizing and saying, "It doesn't apply to me," or, "What can I do?" Yet Christians can incorporate and tolerate harsh business practices even in their own enterprises. Firing people close to retirement, unfair treatment of women in salary policies, and other injustices can exist unless we change how we treat people.

The conditions that James is describing may seem hopeless. Many of the rich will not repent. Believers can live with hope, however, because Christ is coming back. He will bring judgment and justice. It is to Christ's return that James now turns.

PATIENCE IN SUFFERING / 5:7-12

The believers, most of whom were poor, were frequently exploited by the rich and were persecuted because of their faith. This external pressure led to problems in the church as their frustration reached the boiling point. James encouraged the believers to be patient until the Lord's return. But the patience he describes is not passive. It is a patience that involves action:

- Firm perseverance in the face of trials

- Loving and caring for one another in the church

- Refusing to criticize or grumble against other believers

- Praying for the sick

- Confessing sin

- Bringing back any who wander from the faith

Each believer clearly had much to do to keep his or her own lifestyle, behavior, and speech in line with what James was teaching. James's entire letter called those believers, and calls us, to right behavior.

In this section, James illustrates some helpful sources for personal application. After speaking of the need for patience, he proceeds to reveal a number of different lessons that reinforce and apply his theme. The principle of patience will not mean much unless we can apply it to our lives. By looking at life through James's eyes, we discover there are many ways God gives us guidance and encouragement. From his examples we learn the following approaches:

- To observe the processes God has included in nature and use them to think about how God works in human lives (5:7, the autumn and spring rains)

- To observe the processes required for good work in the world and use them to think about ways God wants us to work at life (5:7, the patience required in farming)

- To observe specific lessons in Scripture and use them to think about our behavior in the world (5:8-9, the warning not to grumble)

- To observe the lives of others who have been obedient to God and use them to think about better ways to obey God (5:10, the prophets)

5:7 **Be patient.** James again directs his remarks to his brothers in Christ. The patience that he calls for requires them to wait under duress. James tells his brothers to be patient, even in the midst of injustice. The believers need to endure, trust in God through their trials, and refuse to try to get even for wrongs committed against them (see also 1:2, 12; Psalm 37). But patience does not mean inaction. There is work to be done—serving God, caring for one another, and proclaiming the Good News.

> Don't judge the Lord by his unfinished work. Be patient till he unveils the perfect pattern in glory. Await the "end of the Lord." *F. B. Meyer*

Until the coming of the Lord.^{NKJV} There is an end point, a time when patience will no longer be needed—the Lord's coming. At that time, everything will be made right. The early church lived in constant expectation of Christ's return, and so should we. Because we don't know when Christ will return to bring justice and remove oppression, we must wait with patience (see 2 Peter 3:8-10).

Generations have come and gone, yet the Lord's coming is still on the horizon. Patience is still expected of believers. We are asked in Hebrews to consider the generations of faithful men and women who lived before Christ: "All these people were still living by faith when they died. They did not receive the things promised; they only saw them and welcomed them from a distance. And they admitted that they were aliens and strangers on earth" (Hebrews 11:13 NIV). The faith of those people was based on God's character and promise. In addition, our faith is based on the foundation of Jesus himself, the fulfillment of the promise. Knowing that Christ has come once, just as promised, we should be able to wait patiently and actively for his next coming.

As an example of patience, James talks about the farmer who must wait for his "valuable crop." (NIV) He prepares the field, waits for the "autumn rain" (NIV) as part of sowing the seed, cares for the growing crop, and then waits for the "spring rain" (NIV) as the crop ripens. In Israel the autumn rain comes in October or November after the seed is planted; the "spring rain" (NIV) comes in March or April just before harvesttime. Those who live in arid places understand the remarkable effect of a single rain. The seasons can change in a day, almost before someone's eyes. As the rain falls, dried trees come to life and parched ground springs into bloom. James actually calls these the "early" and "latter" rains (NKJV), using an expression for an ideal growing season. Patience is what must be exercised and developed between the rains. Even nonfarmers have plenty of opportunities to develop patience.

The waiting for the arrival of a baby, starting a new job, finishing school, waiting for a loved one's visit, slowly improving health during a prolonged illness—all these situations try our patience. We will exercise patience as we concentrate on the end result of our waiting. God's way is seldom the quick way, but it is always the complete way.

WHY WAIT?

The farmer must wait patiently for his crops to grow; he cannot hurry the process. But he does not take the summer off and hope that all goes well in the fields. There is much work to do to ensure a good harvest. In the same way, we must wait patiently for Christ's return. We cannot make him come back any sooner. But while we wait, there is much work we can do to advance God's kingdom. Both farmers and Christians must live by faith, looking toward the future reward for their labors. Don't live as if Christ will never come. Work faithfully to build his kingdom—the King *will* come when the time is ripe.

5:8 **Stand firm.**[NIV] Standing firm is difficult in the face of temptation, persecution, problems, trials, and suffering. This challenging phrase literally means "be patient and strengthen your hearts" (see also 1 Thessalonians 3:13; 2 Thessalonians 2:17). Instead of being like the rich people of verse 5 who have "fattened" their hearts on the wealth of this world, believers are to allow the assurance of Christ's return to strengthen their hearts. The English words *stand firm* are used because they convey the meaning of *sterizo*, which could also be translated "establish" or "confirm." Again, consider the heart: a strong, steady heartbeat characterizes a healthy person; a racing or erratic pulse rate is a sure sign of physical trouble. Whatever the circumstances, James encourages us to be rock solid in our faith and to have a faith-inspired joy that permeates every part of life (see 1:2-4).

> Is not the life of man upon earth a trial? Who would want troubles and difficulties? You command us to endure them, not to love them. No person loves what he endures, though he may love the act of enduring.   *Augustine*

The coming of the Lord is near.[NRSV] Like the farmer, we invest a long time in our future hope. The farmer is at the mercy of the weather—it is outside his control. Likewise, the timing of the Lord's return is beyond our control. James believed that Jesus could return in his lifetime. We ought to live with the same conviction. Christ may come back today; at any time, his return may be "near," for we do not know when it will occur (Matthew 24:27, 37, 39; 1 Thessalonians 5:2; 2 Peter 3:10). But we do know that it *will* occur.

STANDING FIRM
Patient obedience can be exercised in some of the following ways:

- Being resolute in our resistance to sin (4:7)
- Contemplating God's grace (Hebrews 13:9)
- Encouraging one another (Hebrews 10:25)
- Continuing to serve others, doing good deeds (Hebrews 10:24)
- Focusing on our eventual meeting with Christ (4:13-17)
- Disregarding pain and criticism (Hebrews 12:1-4)

5:9 Do not grumble against one another. NKJV These believers, facing persecution from the outside and problems on the inside, may naturally find themselves grumbling and criticizing one another. James doesn't want them to be filled with resentment and bitterness toward each other—that would only destroy the unity they so desperately need. Refraining from grumbling is part of what it means to be patient (5:7).

James combines the highest standard of expected behavior with a true understanding of how people often behave. Each time he focuses on a significant pattern of behavior, he almost immediately turns to a human reaction that will undermine the process if it is not confronted. In a similar passage (4:11), James follows his appeal about the importance of submitting to God with a warning about brothers slandering one another. Here he turns from the importance of patience to the danger of grumbling. Is it not profoundly human to avoid facing a weakness in ourselves by pointing to the same weakness in others? In this case, people who are struggling with their lack of patience can always find an example or two of someone who is even less patient than they are! But blaming others instead of facing our sins leaves us open to the judgment of God.

TAKING IT OUT ON OTHERS
It is easy to complain during a time of extended trial of our patience. If we keep quiet, our smothered resentment can flare up. It becomes natural to strike out. God calls us to be unnatural. Don't retaliate. Instead, we should remember the nearness of God and be patient.

So that you may not be judged. NRSV Jesus said, "Do not judge, or you too will be judged. For in the same way you judge others, you will be judged, and with the measure you use, it will be measured to you" (Matthew 7:1-2 NIV). He also said, "But I tell you that men will have to give account on the day of judgment for every careless word they have spoken" (Matthew 12:36 NIV). Grumbling against one another indicates a careless attitude of speech. Because of the dangers created by our speech (see James 3:1-12), we cannot afford to be lax in the way we speak to and about each other.

The Judge is standing at the door! NKJV James has already mentioned the Judge (4:12). This Judge is not far away, but is rapidly approaching; in fact, he is a hair's breadth away, on the other side of the door. The appointed day may be approaching, but the Judge is already standing at the door! Christ's return in majesty and glory could happen at any moment, but he is also very much present in believers by his Spirit. James is warning believers not to be in the middle of judging, quarreling, criticizing, or gossiping when the one they should be serving returns (see also Matthew 24:33; Mark 13:29; Philippians 4:5; 1 Thessalonians 5:1-2; 1 Peter 4:7). Knowledge of Christ's presence is not only comforting; it can also be convicting—especially when we begin behaving as if he were far away.

James's imagery here is strikingly similar to John's picture of Jesus confronting the churches in Revelation: "Here I am! I stand at the door and knock. If anyone hears my voice and opens the door, I will come in and eat with him, and he with me" (Revelation 3:20 NIV). In that context, Jesus repeatedly questioned the lives of those who claimed to be his followers. He confronted local churches with their loss of faithfulness. How much better it is for believers and churches to welcome Christ into their midst!

5:10 **As an example of patience in the face of suffering, take the prophets who spoke in the name of the Lord.** NIV Jewish Christians knew the stories of the prophets, many of whom suffered greatly or were killed for proclaiming God's message (for example, see Elijah in 1 Kings 19:1ff; Jeremiah in Jeremiah 38; Amos in Amos 7). James is reminding his readers that even those who spoke in the name of the Lord had to endure suffering. Part of his point is that God does not preserve us *from* suffering that he has called; rather, he preserves them *in* suffering. They are an example to all believers because of their obedience and faithfulness despite the hardships they endured.

When our ready response to suffering is grumbling and complaining, we reveal our misunderstanding of what God promises

PERSECUTED PROPHETS

Prophet	Persecution	Passage
MOSES	The Israelites complained and rebelled against Moses because they were in the desert and had no water.	Exodus 17:1-7
DAVID	King Saul persecuted David because David was becoming a powerful leader, threatening Saul's position.	1 Samuel 20-27 Psalms 31:13; 59:1-4
VARIOUS PROPHETS	Jezebel killed many of God's prophets because she didn't like having her evil ways pointed out.	1 Kings 18:3-4
ELIJAH	Elijah had to flee for his life when he confronted King Ahab and Queen Jezebel with their sins.	1 Kings 18:10-19:2
MICAIAH	King Ahab thought Micaiah was stirring up trouble rather than prophesying from God, so he threw Micaiah into prison.	2 Chronicles 18:12-27
ELISHA	A king of Israel threatened persecution for Elisha because he thought Elisha had caused a famine.	2 Kings 6:31
ZECHARIAH	Zechariah was executed by King Joash because he confronted the people of Judah for disregarding God's Word.	2 Chronicles 24:20-22
JEREMIAH	King Zedekiah thought Jeremiah was a traitor for prophesying Jerusalem's fall, so he had Jeremiah thrown in prison, then into a muddy cistern.	Jeremiah 37:1-38:13
DANIEL	The national leaders caught Daniel praying, so Daniel was thrown into a den of lions.	Daniel 6

to do. When we are tempted to believe that patience is impossible, God reminds us of those who did endure with patience the trials he allowed into their lives. We may take or refuse to take them as an example, but we are not allowed to claim that patience is impossible.

5:11   As you know. NIV What we know, we can remember; what we can remember, we can use for encouragement and application. When we lack an awareness of the history and teaching in the Bible, we have little to fall back on in suffering. History is filled with accounts of those who have suffered extreme deprivation and had to rely on their memories of the Scriptures. Many have confessed that they wished they had learned more of the Bible while there was leisure to learn. Here James is leading his readers to apply the lessons from Old Testament lives. For instance, Job may offer us a fascinating look at ancient history and an interesting biography, but Job's best work is as a teacher: one who has suffered and can help us cope with suffering. His life is an example we need to follow.

> No one ought to be confident in his own strength when he undergoes temptation. For whenever we endure evils courageously, our long-suffering comes from Christ.   *Augustine*

We consider blessed those who have persevered. NIV The perseverance of God's prophets may have led them to horrible deaths, and the people of the time may have seen them as cursed—but we now consider them blessed. Jesus said, "Blessed are you when people insult you, persecute you and falsely say all kinds of evil against you because of me. Rejoice and be glad, because great is your reward in heaven, for in the same way they persecuted the prophets who were before you" (Matthew 5:11-12 NIV).

Beyond vague spiritual overtones, what does it mean to be blessed? The background to the English word is almost entirely religious, having to do with ceremonies or indications of God's approval. The Greek verb *makarizo* can also be used to mean "fortunate" or "happy," although neither of those terms carries the same spiritual weight in English as the word *blessed.* It is helpful to think of being blessed as having or sensing God's approval and acceptance. In this way, we could paraphrase this verse: "We consider approved by God those who have persevered." It is not a wasted effort to pause for a moment and imagine the deep sense of well-being a person experiences in knowing that he or she has been approved by God.

> Job's is no groveling, passive, unquestioning submission; Job struggled and questioned, and sometimes even defied, but the flame of faith was never extinguished in his heart.
>
> *William Barclay*

James seems to shift his emphasis in this verse from patience to perseverance, but the shift is a natural one. Perseverance is patience stretched out. Only tested patience deserves the title of perseverance. James is coming full circle to the original thoughts in this letter. Perseverance is an advanced result of the testing of faith (see 1:2-4, 12). Throughout Scripture, perseverance is required of all believers. For example, "All men will hate you because of me, but he who stands firm to the end will be saved" (Matthew 10:22 NIV); "By standing firm you will gain life" (Luke 21:19; see also 1 Corinthians 9:24-27; Philippians 3:13-14; 2 Timothy 4:6-8).

You have heard of Job's perseverance. NIV Job may have complained, but he did not stop trusting or obeying God (see Job 1:21; 2:10; 16:19-21; 19:25-27). And the Lord did deliver and restore him (see Job 42:12). The believers, after all the suffering they had endured thus far, were encouraged not to give up—God would deliver and reward them.

What the Lord finally brought about. NIV In an age of instant solutions and results, how the word *finally* grinds against our will. We would much rather read "quickly" or "immediately" than be reminded again that God's timing and priorities are different from ours. But perseverance is never instantaneous. There are no shortcuts to what the Lord brings about; the pathway before us is perseverance. Any explanation of the Christian faith that overlooks or denies the importance of perseverance will disappoint those who believe it.

We can see clearly from Job's life that perseverance is not the result of understanding. Job never received an explanation from God for his suffering. This is partly because pain is often a part of life that must be endured beyond explanations. There are many things we can understand, but not everything. God's purpose is not that we just develop a mind full of explanations and answers; his purpose is to bring us to a place where we trust him.

The Lord is very compassionate and merciful. NKJV God does not enjoy watching his people suffer. He allows them to face such pain because a greater good will be produced. Some who have suffered a great deal more than any of us have unashamedly praised God: "Because of the LORD'S great love we are not consumed, for his compassions never fail" (Lamentations 3:22 NIV; see also Psalm 103:8; 111:4). In the meantime, James encourages his readers to trust in God, wait patiently, persevere, and remember God's incredible love, compassion, and mercy for his people. Here, as in 2:13, when James has led us to a place of real challenge, he makes the challenge possible by adding the hope of God's mercy. Left with our own resources, perseverance is beyond us. Our trust in God must combine the desire to persevere and the willingness to receive God's help. God can help us persevere. He can even help us want to persevere. But he will not force us to persevere if that is not our desire. "For it is God who is at work in you, enabling you both to will and to work for his good pleasure" (Philippians 2:13 NRSV).

5:12 Do not swear. James is referring to Jesus' words in Matthew 5:34-37. To swear means to make an oath. Making oaths was a common practice, and James wanted it discontinued among the believers. People made disrespectful or arrogant verbal guarantees that they themselves could reverse by legal technicalities. Like boldfaced warranties with lots of fine print, these oaths were intended to create an impression of truth—but those who uttered them did not really expect to be held to them. Christians should not need to use oaths in order to guarantee the truth of what they say. Our honesty should be unquestionable.

Should we take oaths in court? The oaths forbidden here are those used in casual conversation, not formal oaths taken in a court of law. Legal oaths are intended to bind those who make them. Perjury is a serious offense. Most scholars conclude that James does not require us to refuse to take oaths in court. The swearing that so irritated Jesus and James made a mockery of the truth.

The foundational principle behind these concerns is rooted in the third commandment, "You shall not misuse the name of the LORD your God, for the LORD will not hold anyone guiltless who misuses his name" (Exodus 20:7 NIV). We can see the danger of judgment in the flippant use of God's name in our society. The blatant lack of respect for God and for Jesus is crystallized in their names' being reduced to expletives. Those who don't like that kind of language get labelled as "sensitive listeners." We must not accept the label. Believers need to realize that this lack of respect is probably at least as often due to ignorance as to willful disobedience. One way to find out is to ask the person if he isn't sometimes afraid when he casually uses the Lord's name. If the question raises curiosity about why on earth he or she should be afraid, a simple quoting of the third commandment might start an interesting ongoing discussion.

Let your "Yes" be yes, and your "No," no, or you will be condemned. NIV Believers should not need oaths, for their speech should always be truthful. There should be no reason for them to have to strengthen a statement with an oath. God will judge our words.

A person with a reputation for exaggeration or lying often can't get anyone to believe him on his word alone. For example, this person might say, "I promise!" or "I swear!" Christians should never become like that. Always be honest so that others will believe your simple "yes" or "no." By avoiding lies, half-truths, and omissions of the truth, you will become known as a trustworthy person.

FAITHFUL PRAYER / 5:13-18

James closes his letter as he began it, with a call to prayer. In 1:5, after an opening challenge about joy in trials (which can easily be shown as a description of prayers of praise), he urges believers specifically to pray for the wisdom they need in becoming mature. James informs us that God will give generously that kind of wisdom without blaming us for our lack. The sole requirement is a faithful trust in God's supply. Later, in 4:1-3, James addresses the kind of selfish prayers that God does not answer. His confrontation is unmistakable: "When you ask, you do not receive, because you ask with wrong motives, that you may spend what you get on your pleasures" (4:3 NIV). Prayer is an essential tool, but it cannot be used to manipulate God.

James uses his closing words to describe effective prayer. He details prayer in several forms (praise, intercession, confession) and connects prayer with several other important spiritual disciplines (healing, confession, anointing, correction, praise, and mutual forgiveness). If we can say that James's letter summarizes the work of faith, his conclusion focuses on faith's finest work—believers effective in prayer.

5:13 Are any among you suffering? They should pray. NRSV There are many responses to trouble. Some of us worry; some of us vow revenge against those who have caused the trouble; some of us let anger burn inside us. Some grumble. But James says the correct response to trouble is to pray (see also Psalm 30; 50:15; 91:15). This is not necessarily a prayer for deliverance from the trouble, but for the patience and strength to endure it.

There are three main reasons for not praying when we realize we are in trouble: ignorance, arrogance, and shame. If we do not know that God wants us to pray when we are in trouble, we are simply ignorant of Scripture. If we do not pray when we are in trouble because we are trusting in our own resources to get ourselves out, we are being arrogant. And sometimes we may want to pray but are ashamed because the trouble we are in is our own fault. James gives permission and encouragement to those who are ignorant. He urges submission to those who are arrogant. And he reminds those who are ashamed that God is full of compassion and mercy (5:11). To all of us he commends prayer.

Are any cheerful? They should sing songs of praise. NRSV James says that if we are fortunate enough to be happy, we should thank God by singing songs of praise (see also 1 Corinthians 14:15; Ephesians 5:19; Colossians 3:16). Because our praise is directed to God, singing is actually another form of prayer. These songs of praise can be the formal Psalms from the Old Testament, or spontaneous personal creations that express some aspect of God's character or our response to him.

THE BENEFIT OF SINGING

Almost every Sunday, we unconsciously apply James 5:13. The use of hymn singing in worship is not merely to create a mood, allow people to stand and stretch, or provide a break between the spoken parts—hymn singing is a form of prayer. It ought to be composed, played, and sung with devotion. We should think of what we are singing and sing with joyful reverence. Whether it is our song, or one composed by another, our expression of the words ought to be genuine. By its nature, music allows us to come as close as possible to praising God in perfect union. Perhaps not every person is happy, but the joyful expression of a few may actually be what God uses to lift the spirits of those who are broken or lost.

The quicker we are to blame God for misfortune, the slower we are to praise God when good things happen. Some of us take our happiness too lightly. We accept it as if it is our due or simply the product of our efforts. In happiness, it is easy to forget God. But a real appreciation of happy times will lead us to recognizing their source. If prayer is to be our constant communication with God, then happy times should naturally add rhythm and music to our expressions of thanks and praise to him.

5:14 **Are any among you sick? They should call for the elders.** NRSV One characteristic of the early church was its concern over and care for the sick. Here James encourages the sick person to call for the elders of the church for counseling and prayer. The elders were spiritually mature men who were responsible for overseeing local churches (see 1 Peter 5:1-4). These men would **pray over** the sick person, calling upon the Lord for healing. Then they would **anoint him with oil in the name of the Lord** (NIV). Jesus himself instructed us to pray in his name (John 14:14). As the elders pray for this one who is sick, they are to voice clearly that the power for healing resides in the name of Jesus.

Many of the details in this passage have to be consciously applied in our own age. James wrote to people in rather small communities, bound tightly by language and culture. We live in communities marked by isolation—even from people living next door. The early church practiced house calls. Contact, prayer, appeals to the presence and power of God, expectations of God's direct intervention, and healing were part of daily life. The life of faith really was a lifestyle, not a weekend component of a compartmentalized life that fits God into one's weekly schedule for a couple of hours on Sunday mornings. A literal practice by church leaders of James's guidelines for healing prayer would make churches much more personal and effective.

The sick person here is incapacitated physically. Anointing was often used by the early church in their prayers for healing. In Scripture, oil was both a medicine (see the parable of the Good Samaritan in Luke 10:30-37) and a symbol of the Spirit of God (as used in anointing kings; see 1 Samuel 16:1-13). Thus the oil may have been a sign of the power of prayer, and it may have symbolized the setting apart of the sick person for God's special attention.

More important than the oil itself, however, the key function of the elders is their prayer for the sick person, as evidenced in the verses that follow.

USE OF OIL

Many ceremonies and actions (such as fasting and baptism) were so well known among the early Christians that specific instructions are not always included. The same is true with anointing. We don't know what kind of oil this was, or how exactly it was administered. The only hint we get is a delightful description in one of the Psalms that fits nicely with the themes that James is emphasizing here: "How good and pleasant it is when brothers live together in unity! It is like precious oil poured on the head, running down on the beard, running down on Aaron's beard, down upon the collar of his robes. It is as if the dew of Hermon were falling on Mount Zion. For there the Lord bestows his blessing, even life forevermore" (Psalm 133:1-3 NIV).

5:15 **The prayer offered in faith will make the sick person well.**NIV The prayer must be from the heart, sincere, with trust in and obedience to God behind it, and with no doubting, as in 1:5-8. The believing is the role of the elders who are praying, not the sick person's (nothing is said about his or her faith). It is possible that the sick person's faith is exercised in calling the elders. Also, if there is need for confession, the elders will be able to minister to the individual. The process insures dependence of believers on each other.

The Lord will raise him up.[NKJV] Not the elders or the oil, but the Lord himself does the healing. Does this mean that every prayer for healing guarantees that God will make the sick person well? It must be emphasized here that the prayer offered is a prayer offered in faith—not only the faith that believes God can heal, but also the faith that expresses absolute confidence in God's will. A true prayer of faith will acknowledge God's sovereignty in his answer to that prayer. It is not always God's will to heal those who are ill (see 2 Corinthians 12:7-9). A prayer for healing must be qualified with a recognition that God's will is supreme.

It is shameful to find Christians hesitating to pray because God might not heal the way they wish. It is not our role either to decide how God will answer our prayers or to excuse him if our human desires are not met. Trusting God only as long as he cooperates with our plans is no trust at all. The prayer offered in faith gives God a free hand to work. Because believers have an eternal viewpoint, we can claim the absolute certainty of this promise—God can and will heal, though not always in this world. In the afterlife God "will wipe every tear from their eyes. There will be no more death or mourning or crying or pain, for the old order of things has passed away" (Revelation 21:4 NIV). To limit God's answers only to this world would indicate that we are trying to make God submit to our needs and desires in this life rather than submitting to him.

WHAT ABOUT WEAK FAITH?
The emphasis on the prayer offered in faith in James gives rise to questions such as, Does the quality of faith matter? What if my faith is too weak? What if not enough elders show up? What if the elders' faith is weak? Or even, I was completely confident God would answer my prayer, but the person wasn't healed—what did I do wrong?

These are important questions. Sometimes prayer is offered for the sick with the hope that a specific healing request will come true. Our prayers should always connect those in need with God, who can be depended on to do what is best.

Jesus chided human attempts to measure faith. He pictured the strongest faith as no bigger than a mustard seed. To the disciples' questions about unanswered prayers Jesus replied, "Because you have so little faith. I tell you the truth, if you have faith as small as a mustard seed, you can say to this mountain, 'Move from here to there' and it will move. Nothing will be impossible for you" (Matthew 17:20 NIV). Clearly the size of our faith in God is not important; rather, it is the character of the God in whom our faith rests that makes the difference.

An overemphasis on our faith's involvement places too much responsibility on our capacity to know God's plan in the matter. But if we have a small faith that simply trusts in a wise, merciful, and powerful God to do what is best, we will see miracles happen.

If he has sinned, he will be forgiven. NIV Sin may or may not be the cause of the illness, but an opportunity for confession is given, and the elders are there to receive it. No demand of confession is given; James uses the word "if." This condition is important because all too often we are prone to assume that sin is the cause of someone's suffering. The Bible teaches that sin can cause sickness (see Mark 2:1-12; 1 Corinthians 5:5; 11:27-30), but it also notes clearly that this is not always the case (see John 9:2-3).

5:16 Confess your sins to one another and pray for one another. NRSV It is not God's plan that his people be alone. Members of Christ's body should be able to count on others for support and prayer, especially when they are sick or suffering. The elders should be on call to respond to the illness of any member, and the church should stay alert to pray for the healing of any who are sick. But we are often not only guilty of hesitating to lean on each other in our sicknesses and weaknesses. We are even more liable not to confess our sins to each other.

Fellowship in our churches could be vastly improved if we could follow James's formula here. Confessing our sins—such as resentment, a grudge, lack of forgiveness, etc.—can and often does lead to the healing of physical ailments. Unresolved anger and guilt create real stress. If

More things are wrought
   by prayer
Than this world dreams
   of.
Wherefore, let their
   voice
Rise like a fountain for
   me night and day.
For what are men better
   than sheep or goats
That nourish a blind life
   within the brain,
If, knowing God, they lift
   not hands of prayer
Both for themselves and
   those who call them
   friend?
For so the whole round
   earth is every way
Bound by gold chains
   about the feet of
   God.
       Tennyson

a believer could freely confess sin to someone whom he or she has wronged, confess publicly to the entire church if needed, or confess in private (if more appropriate), and then have the church pray for him or her, the barriers that are erected between people could be torn down. There would no longer be the internal conflicts, and fellowship would be strong and supportive. Those who are sick **may be healed** (NRSV), and the church would be unified in its prayer efforts.

The recent emphasis on small groups within churches has risen largely from a need to recapture some of these basic features of life in the body of Christ that have been neglected. When Christians are really working to "carry each other's burdens," the world does take note, and we come closer to fulfilling "the law of Christ" (see Galatians 6:2 NIV). Loving your neighbor as yourself does include, above all else, praying for him or her.

WHY CONFESS SIN?

Christ has made it possible for us to go directly to God for forgiveness. But confessing our sins to one another still has an important place in the life of the church.

- If we have sinned against an individual, we must ask that person to forgive us.
- If our sin has affected the church, we must confess it publicly.
- If we need loving support as we struggle with a sin, we should confess the sin to those who are able to provide that support.
- If after confessing a private sin to God we still don't feel his forgiveness, we may wish to confess that sin to a fellow believer and hear him or her assure us of God's pardon.

In Christ's kingdom, every believer is a priest to other believers (1 Peter 2:9). We must help others come to Christ and tell them of Christ's forgiveness.

The prayer of the righteous is powerful and effective. NRSV The prayer is effective because the person who is praying is righteous. The person is not sinless, but he or she has confessed known sins to God and is completely committed to him and trying to do his will. Again, we can say that the righteous person gets what he or she wants in prayer because he wants what God wants.

The Christian's most powerful resource is communication with God through prayer. It is the instrument of healing and forgiveness and is a mighty weapon for spiritual warfare. The results are often greater than we thought were possible. Some people see prayer as a last resort, to be tried when all else fails. Our priorities are the reverse of God's. Prayer should come first. Some see prayer as a way to obligate God to give whatever they claim in faith. God is pleased to use our prayers to accomplish his purposes and he delights in answering our needs, but he is never bound by our prayers. God's power is infinitely greater than ours, so it only makes sense to rely on it—especially because God encourages us to do so.

5:17-18 Elijah was . . . like us. NRSV Prayer is indeed powerful—remember Elijah? The story is found in 1 Kings 17:1–18:46. Elijah had great power in prayer. A drought came as a sign to evil King Ahab of Israel that the idol Baal did not have power over the rain, God did. And when Elijah prayed, **it did not rain on the land for three and a half years.** Then he prayed for rain, **and the heavens gave rain** (NIV).

James uses Old Testament people to illustrate each of his major themes:

- The nature of faith is found in the lives of Abraham and Rahab (2:21-25).

- Perseverance is exemplified by Job (5:11).

- Effective prayer is exemplified by Elijah (5:17-18).

These lives are important to us. They are examples to be followed. When we choose all our models from contemporary people, we may eventually be disappointed by their failures. Other generations of believers cannot let us down. They made their mistakes, persevered, and are now testimonies that life can be lived for God. Hebrews reminds us, "Since we are surrounded by such a great cloud of witnesses, let us throw off everything that hinders and the sin that so easily entangles, and let us run with perseverance the race marked out for us" (Hebrews 12:1).

ELIJAH WAS LIKE US
Elijah was human, a follower of God who sometimes got depressed or had doubts. He snatched defeat out of the jaws of victory when he ran from Jezebel after decisively crushing the prophets of Baal. But James uses Elijah as an example of someone who did not allow his own weaknesses to undermine his trust in God. Elijah's weak belief in himself forced him to believe even more firmly in God. James is inviting us to identify with Elijah's weakness so that we might develop the same honesty and power in prayer that Elijah exercised. The same God who listened to and acted on Elijah's prayers will give attention to ours.

RESTORE WANDERING BELIEVERS / 15:19-20

Behind this question about the identity of the wanderer is a pastoral concern. In practice, it makes no difference whether the wanderer was actually a believer or not—we are commanded to attempt to turn the person back to the faith (see Ezekiel 3:18-21; 33:9; 1 Timothy 4:16). If the wanderer should die while wandering, the pastor or group is left to wonder about the eternal state of that person. Families sometimes agonize over the fate of a loved one who has wandered away from the faith. Frankly, we cannot know. To determine what was really occurring within that person we would have to be God. If we have done what we could to reach out to wanderers while they were still living, we must then turn their eternal destiny over to God. James urges Christians to help backsliders return to God. By taking the initiative, praying for the person, and acting in love, we can meet the person where he or she is and encourage his or her return to God.

5:19 **If one among you wanders from the truth.** NKJV By saying *one among you,* James is referring to a believer who has fallen away from the faith by becoming involved with idolatry or heresy. He also reminds us that no one in the group is immune from wandering. The *one* could be us. To *wander* means a serious departure from the faith— otherwise known as "apostasy." The Greek word is *planete,* (from which we get our word "planet"); it suggests wandering away from the correct path. It means wandering, like Pilgrim in *The Pilgrim's Progress,* from the right path onto another path that will lead only to destruction. *Truth,* as used here, does not refer to peripheral doctrinal concerns, but to the central truth of the Christian faith—namely, that Jesus is the Son of God, the Lord and Savior who died for our sins and rose again from the dead. Choices and actions that lead us towards denying the lordship of the living Christ carry us away from the truth.

WHAT IS TRUTH?
- The truth is *lived* as well as *believed* (John 3:21).
- Jesus' teaching is the truth; and when we know the truth, he, the truth, sets us free (John 8:31-32).
- The truth is a gift of the Holy Spirit, who is the spirit of truth and who guides us to the truth (John 16:13).
- Jesus came into the world to testify of the truth; we have the truth when we listen to him (John 18:37).
- We are called to obey the truth (Galatians 5:7), speak the truth in love (Ephesians 4:15), and love the truth (2 Thessalonians 2:10).
- We love with actions and in truth, and by doing so, we know we belong to the truth (1 John 3:18-19).

And someone should bring him back.[NIV] When someone does wander, the church or Christian community ought to try to bring him back, not for judgment, but for repentance and restoration. But this phrase also has a distinct personal application, for the *group* is represented by *someone*. When a believer is aware of another believer's wandering, that knowledge carries with it responsibility for action. All these images portray a community where people care deeply for each other, and wanderers are not allowed to slip through the cracks unnoticed. Are we willing to try to bring back someone who has wandered, or do we simply wring our hands while the person goes off into darkness?

5:20   Remember this: Whoever turns a sinner from the error of his way will save him from death and cover over a multitude of sins.[NIV] The error of the wandering sinner is so serious as to lead to death—spiritual, eternal death—if he or she is not brought back (see 1 Corinthians 11:30; 1 John 5:16). But when the believer repents and returns to God, God will forgive, cover over, and forget that person's sins (see Psalm 32:1; 1 Peter 4:8).

The context is somewhat unclear about the identity of the wanderer. Is it a person who is a believer wandering away, or is it a person in the group who has not truly believed and is wandering away? Christians disagree over whether or not it is possible for people to lose their salvation, but all agree that those who move away from their faith or who are not genuine in their profession are in serious trouble and need to repent. The point of this verse is clear, though: we are to bring the wanderer back—not debate whether or not the person would be lost if we didn't.

What began with a challenge to endure hardship with joy now closes with an appeal to watch out for each other. Believers are to pursue their faith, together. It is God who saves and keeps, but he allows us to be involved in one another's Christian life.

It is an unforgettable sight to witness the Christian welcome of someone who has strayed and returned, watching God's forgiveness work through the body of Christ as believers accept the person who is repenting. From the view of eternity, it must really be like a cover being pulled over a "multitude of sins." James has repeatedly instructed us that Christians should not grumble against each other and judge each other. When we pray for each other and speak God's forgiveness to each other, we, the church, experience and demonstrate the life Christ gave us. God promises that what has been covered by forgiveness will be remembered no more. "For I will forgive their wickedness and will remember their sins no more" (Jeremiah 31:34).

FAITH THAT WORKS

James offers a larger number of similarities to the Sermon on the Mount than any other book in the New Testament. James relied heavily on Jesus' teachings.

Lesson	Reference
When your life is full of difficulties and persecutions, be happy. A reward awaits you.	James 1:2 Matthew 5:10-12
You are to be perfect, strong in character, full, and complete.	James 1:4 Matthew 5:48
Ask God and he will answer.	James 1:5; 5:15 Matthew 7:7-12
Those who are humble, who don't amount to much by the world's standards, should be very glad.	James 1:9 Matthew 5:3
Watch out for your anger . . . it can be dangerous.	James 1:20 Matthew 5:22
Be merciful to others, as God is merciful to you.	James 2:13 Matthew 5:7; 6:14
Your faith must be proven by your care for others.	James 2:14-16 Matthew 7:21-23
Happy are those who strive for peace; peacemakers plant seeds of peace and reap a harvest of goodness.	James 3:17-18 Matthew 5:9
You cannot serve God and money, pleasures, or evil. Friendship with evil makes you an enemy of God.	James 4:4 Matthew 6:24
When we humble ourselves and realize our need for God, he will come to us and encourage us.	James 4:10 Matthew 5:3-4
Don't criticize or speak evil of others; it works against God's command to love one another.	James 4:11 Matthew 7:1-2
Treasures on earth will only erode and disappear—we must store eternal treasures in heaven.	James 5:2 Matthew 6:19
Be patient in suffering, as God's prophets were patient.	James 5:10 Matthew 5:10-12
Be honest in your speech so you can say a simple yes or no and always be trusted	James 5:12 Matthew 5:33-37

The letter of James is Christianity with its sleeves rolled up. It is the working person's practical guide to living the Christian faith. It spells out what it means to follow Jesus day by day. James emphasizes faith in action. Theories are for theologians, but James is interested in life! Right living is the evidence and result of faith. The church must serve with compassion, speak lovingly and truthfully, live in obedience to God's commands, and love one another. The body of believers ought to be an example of heaven's principles applied on earth, drawing people to Christ through love for God and one another. If we truly believe God's Word, we will *live it* day by day. God's Word is not merely something we read or think about, but something we do.

BIBLIOGRAPHY

Adamson, James B. *The Epistle of James*. The New International Commentary on the New Testament. Grand Rapids: Eerdmans, 1976.

Barclay, William. *The Letters of James and Peter*. Philadelphia: Westminster, 1961.

Bowman, John W. *The Letter of James*. The Layman's Bible Commentary 24. Atlanta: John Knox Press, 1962.

Burdick, Donald W. *James*. Expositor's Bible Commentary. Vol. 12. Editor Frank E. Gaebelein. Grand Rapids: Zondervan, 1981.

Davids, Peter H. *James*. New International Biblical Commentary. Peabody, Massachusetts: Hendrickson Publishers, 1989.

Douglas, J. D. and Philip Comfort (editors). *New Commentary on the Whole Bible: New Testament*. Wheaton: Tyndale House Publishers, 1990.

Hughes, Robert B. and J. Carl Laney. *New Bible Companion*. Wheaton: Tyndale House Publishers, 1990.

Hughes, R. Kent. *James: Faith that Works*. Wheaton: Crossway Books, Good News Publishers, 1991.

Martin, Ralph. *James*. Word Biblical Commentary. Waco, Texas: Word Books, 1988.

Meyer, Frederick B. *Bible Commentary*. Wheaton: Tyndale House Publishers, 1979.

Moo, Doug. *James*. Tyndale New Testament Commentary, revised. Grand Rapids: Eerdmans, 1988.

Tasker, R. V. G. *The General Epistle of James*. Tyndale New Testament Commentary. London: Tyndale Press, 1956.

Walvoord, John F. and Roy B. Zuck. *The Bible Knowledge Commentary: New Testament Edition*. Wheaton: Victor Books, Scripture Press Publications, 1983.

INDEX